I0832337

THE TRAGEDIAN;

AN ESSAY ON

THE HISTRIONIC GENIUS

OF

JUNIUS BRUTUS BOOTH.

BY

THOMAS R. GOULD.

NEW YORK:
PUBLISHED BY HURD AND HOUGHTON.
Cambridge: Riverside Press.
1868.

RIVERSIDE, CAMBRIDGE:
STEREOTYPED AND PRINTED BY
H. O. HOUGHTON AND COMPANY.

To

EDWIN BOOTH,

WHOSE RARE GOOD GIFTS HAVE ALREADY WON FOR HIM
THE UNDIVIDED ADMIRATION AND RESPECT OF
HIS COUNTRYMEN,

These Memorials

OF HIS ILLUSTRIOUS FATHER, ARE AFFECTIONATELY
INSCRIBED,

BY THE AUTHOR.

PUBLISHER'S NOTE.

THE admirable photograph which faces the title-page, was taken by H. G. Smith from a marble bust of Mr. Booth, sculptured by the author of this volume.

CONTENTS.

THE TRAGEDIAN.

DECEMBER, 1852.

TEN days ago a private letter from New Orleans assured us, that the great actor of the age had arrived from the "Golden Land," was then playing an engagement in that city, and appeared in remarkably good health.

Swiftly following this intelligence — which gave us hope soon again to "have sight" of the Proteus of Shakespearean character "coming from the sea," and hear once more the strange inward music of his voice — came last week, with "spleen of speed," the telegram that he had died on the passage to Cincinnati.

Our first feeling was the pang of a personal friendship, suddenly parted. Then came the thought that a great artist, the greatest in his sphere in our day, had passed away; and finally, vivid images and emotions, won from that wide range of tragic character in which he so truthfully lived, came crowding into our memory.

JUNIUS BRUTUS BOOTH was born in London, May 1, 1796. He appeared on the London stage at the age of twenty, but has run the greater part of his dramatic career in this country. He was of short stature, but his presence and action were types of manliness and power. His face was cast originally in the antique Roman mould; and even many years after the untoward accident which spoiled its classic outline, it presented, on one occasion, when we were sitting by his side, a singular resemblance to the portraits of Michael Angelo.

No language can do more than recall, to those who have seen him in his most vital moods, the terrible and beautiful meaning of his look and gesture; or the charm of his massive and resonant voice. For voice, gesture, and every fibre of his wonderful organization, were subordinated to a genius, which laid hold of and expressed, with absolute sincerity, the radical elements of character; and gave play to its minor mani-

OBITUARY.

THOMAS R. GOULD.

The well-known sculptor, Thomas R. Gould, who died Saturday at his home in Florence, was born in Boston 63 years ago. For some time he was engaged in business with his brother John, now living in New-Orleans. His first figure was modeled in the studio of Seth Cheney, his first and only master. After the war he went abroad with his family to study sculpture. At his pleasant home in Florence, where he has since resided, he worked diligently and produced many pieces, among them "The West Wind," "Cleopatra," "Timon of Athens," "Ariel" and "John Hancock," which was exhibited at the Centennial Exposition, and now stands in the Town Hall at Lexington. His statue of Gov. Andrew, which the Grand Army of the Republic commissioned him to produce for erection in the Hingham Cemetery, is one of his well-known works. Two of his ideal studies, "Christ" and "Satan," once formed a part of the Boston Athenæum collection. The "Ghost in Hamlet" and "Steam" and "Electricity," two colossal heads, placed in the vestibule of the Boston *Herald* Building, have been much admired. Among the numerous portrait busts executed by Gould may be mentioned that of Emerson, in the Harvard Library; William Monroe, in the Concord Library; John A. Andrew, belonging to the widow of the statesman, and the elder Booth, in Booth's Theatre, New-York. He was a brother of the late Samuel Gould, of Boston. He visited his native country a few months ago, and was at that time in excellent health.

festations, with the spontaneous freedom and variety of nature.

We well remember how, in former times, we hungered and thirsted, in the intervals of his absence, after the intellectual beauty of his personations.

His great popularity, which time, accident, and eccentric habits seldom availed to diminish, seemed owing mainly to those fire blasts of a volcanic energy, that power of instant and tremendous concentration of passion, which was one constituent of his genius. Yet it was curious to observe a crowded and tumultuous pit, with its new comers struggling for some "coigne of vantage" in the doorways, noisily careless of the sorrows of King Henry, but hushed in a moment,

"Still as night,
Or summer's noontide air,"

as the grand, but subdued and self-communing intonations of Richard's opening soliloquy fell upon their ears.

In the cumulative and energetic evolution of character, which forms the basis of his fame, the subtler traits of Mr. Booth's delineations were often overlooked; but, to our thinking, it was this marvelous delicacy especially which made his acting "the feast it was." It was this rare power which enabled him to follow the lead of Shakespeare's imagination, in its most secret windings and its airiest flights, and found him the sole artist of our time, worthy to present in living form the characters of Hamlet, Iago, Othello, and Lear.

Thus much have we felt impelled to say, in the hurry of the hour, in grateful memory of one from whom we have drawn deep delight and instruction; while we reserve, to some future day, an ampler notice, worthy, we trust, in some measure, of his exalted representative genius.

1868.

An actor's posthumous fame is, by the nature of his art, visionary and traditional. The sculptor's thought lives after him, in lines and masses of imperishable marble; the painter's in simulated forms and "sorcery of color" on his canvas; and from the impish figures of the composer's score, a cunning hand may at any time evoke

"The hidden soul of harmony."

But when a great actor passes away, nothing remains excepting grand and delicate images, which in silent hours crowd the memory of those who have seen him, and the report of which finds a fainter and still receding echo in the minds of those who have not.

In this view, in grateful testimony to the rare delight his personations have afforded; and in the hope of giving body to the vision, and language to the common sentiment of his appreciators, we proceed to record our impressions of Mr. Booth's genius for dramatic impersonation.

And here we feel we cannot advance one steady step without first considering, and haply disposing of, Charles Lamb's thoughtful essay "On the Tragedies of Shakespeare, considered in their fitness for stage representation"; in which he evinces the most penetrating sentiment of the quality of Shakespeare's genius, and denies with equal emphasis, but less discretion, the power of the stage to reproduce it. The sophistry of his argument, as we apprehend it, lies in his applying to Shakespeare's dramas the most subtle imaginative tests, and thereupon assuming the entire absence of the imaginative faculty in the representation of those dramas on the stage. Let us review his theory; for if Shakespeare cannot be represented, it is idle to assign the quality of genius to any actor.

Lamb tells us that, as he was taking a turn in Westminster Abbey, he was struck by an affected figure of Garrick, the player, underwrit by some fustian lines about the equality of genius between Garrick and Shakespeare! Scarcely need we affirm our sympathy with Lamb's condemnation of their "false thoughts and nonsense." They contain sufficient provocation to set off the eccentric genius of Elia at a smart pace in the opposite direction.

We can follow him in his lucid exposition of the inadequacy of the stage to represent supernatural scenery; and the consequent failure of all attempts to reproduce the fairy creations of "A Midsummer Night's Dream," and "The Tempest." These require for their due appreciation, an imagination subtilized by quiet, and airily abstracted from the presence of material objects.

But when he proceeds to distinguish the stage as equally incapable of embodying single human characters, in which the imagination plays a conspicuous part; or who are possessed by supernatural emotions, as Hamlet, Macbeth, Lear, then we part company with the ingenious essayist. The possibility of their adequate representation by living man is involved in the fact of their creation within the sphere of humanity.

No doubt, Lamb's sensitive spirit, developed and nourished in the morning light and dew and fragrance of the English classics, was often shocked by pretenders to the much-abused and misjudged fine art of acting that swarmed the London theatres. Even

Edmund Kean, no pretender, but an original and genuine artist, may have swelled the current of this feeling.

Hazlitt cherished a passionate admiration for Kean; but he was a jealous lover, and frequently chastised his favorite. Kean disappointed him in Lear. The critic quotes the passage,

> "O heavens,
> If you do love old men, if your sweet sway
> Hallow obedience, if yourselves are old,
> Make it your cause; send down, and take my part!
> Art not ashamed to look upon this beard?
> O Regan, wilt thou take her by the hand?"

and adds, "One would think there are tones and looks and gestures answerable to these words, to thrill and harrow up the thoughts, to 'appall the guilty and make mad the free': or that might create a soul under the ribs of death! But we did not see or hear them. It is not enough that Lear's crosses and perplexities are expressed by single strokes."

Lamb retorts, "What have looks and tones to do with that sublime identification of his age with that of the *heavens themselves*, when, in his reproaches to them, for conniving at the injustice of his children, he reminds them that 'they themselves are old'"?

Lamb enforces his abstract point by italicizing the word "heavens." But the attentive reader of the play will see that Lear, the grand old pagan king, uses this word interchangeably with "gods"—the gods were persons if the heavens are not.

The respective printed articles in which these opposing views occur, are the evident outcome of a foregone conversation. We can fancy Hazlitt coming, on a Wednesday evening, hot from the theatre, into that congress of wits and good fellows then assembled at Lamb's lodgings; uttering and controverting opinion, with fierce and fitful eloquence; then disappearing, in order to write one of those papers on Kean's performances, which was to lighten from his firefly page, on the dull world of London, in the "Chronicle" of the following day.

Lamb might have added, and with equal pertinency, to his question about looks and tones, what have *words* to do with that sublime identification? Words are arbitrary signs. Tone is their living spirit. Tone is the direct utterance of the heart and the imagination. We hold with Hazlitt. We have heard tones equal to the expression of the grandest words of Shakespeare. They ring in the chambers of memory. We have seen faces, one face, at least, capable of presenting the very look of Lear, as he stood with his lifted face, blanched and wasted by accumulated and unutterable grief, his soul looking through blue eyes, beyond the storm, towards the blue heavens, the abode of those "kind gods" into whose awful likeness he was for the moment transfigured.

We judge of the capability of an art, had we no better guide, by its best examples, not its average product: as in painting we take, not a tavern sign, being a portrait of the proprietor; but rather Raphael's picture in the Dresden Gallery of that Divine Child whose name is Wonderful.

Lamb supposes that an actor must be thinking only and always of his own appearance. "On what compulsion *must* he? tell us that." A genuine actor, it is true, delights in his own product as an artist; but why may he not feel, at the same time, the inspiration of his author, even to the point of self-forgetfulness? Brooding study, and a mastery over the business of his profession, may be the very means of his emancipation, and contribute to give free play to his genius; even as the habit of virtue deepens the fountains of spontaneous goodness.

Compare for a moment the histrionic with a sister art, and see what delight of liberty the former may command. If the dull and silent clay can be so manipulated by the hand of genius as to insphere and express the rarest beauty of woman, as in that Neapolitan Psyche, pure, proud, visionary; or rise to the colossal grandeur of the Phidian Jupiter, ("how big imagination glows in *that* lip!") why may not the actor, *whose* clay is a living organism of fearful and wonderful forces, make it an instant vehicle of the most glowing inspiration. He is statue, and picture, and poem, and music, and informs them all with life and motion, through the charm of his magnetic presence.

Lamb's article is a special literary plea. Let the closet student exalt, if he will, the pleasure of abstract reverie. We hold it to be "womanish and weak," compared with that robust and intellectual delight, which comes with the "sense of distinctness" a great actor is capable of imparting to creations of human character whose form is genuine, and which can bear light and sound and motion. The charm of Shakespeare's dramas is not a witch's spell, that an uttered word may break.

Certain purists of to-day are following a like line of argument with Lamb, in their graduation of the relative dignity of the arts. Their formula might be stated thus: that is the finest art which employs the most immaterial vehicle. But so long as the beauty of the world depends on the law of gravitation, we dare maintain, that the finest art is that in which the solidest material is permeated by the most spiritual thought. This is the true

"Bridal of the earth and sky."

Not with his usual vision of the germs and processes of genius did Lamb write, that an actor is an imitator of the signs and turns of passion. An actor of the understanding, a *sensible* actor, indeed, always takes this method; an imaginative actor, never. One takes the words of the text (always premising that he is not a poor copy of some empirical precedent), reasons upon, and *infers* the meaning, and so extracts the character. The result of this method, however carefully and comprehensively employed, is at best but an abstract induction, having something of the aspect of reality, but automatic, and without the breath of life.

The other looks, for example, into one of Shakespeare's great creations, as if passing into a real presence; is filled and atmosphered by its spirit; listens to its language as to a living voice; is brought into intimate relations with the springs of its being; and conceives it in unity by the power of a brooding and recreative imagination.

And unto this power, because "it cometh not with observation," but transcends the understanding; because it is vital and life-giving, and elevates acting from a mimetic into an imaginative art, subordinating the comparative intellect to its higher and self-justified laws, we feel bound to give, with a considerate and responsible decision, the sacred name of genius.

This word is too often profaned. We do not intend either to cumber or distract the reader's mind with a new definition. But it will be found equally true of the representative, as of the originating arts, that they find their highest expression with swiftness, ease, and joy. With swiftness; for repose itself, a live quiet, a quality so profound in art and so misappreciated, sits at the farthest remove from dullness, and necessitates a quick continuity of harmonious conditions. "Living" and "quick" are English synonyms. With ease; for, when the high powers of the mind come by invitation or spontaneous consent, and combine and converge towards one common end, the beautiful in art, their grandest and their gravest work is play. The glow of this play is the very element of joy.

If in addition to the power we have indicated, but dare not define, an actor be gifted with an organization instantly responsive to its monitions, the conduit of its influence, and the varying form of its strong possession, or its subtle and shifting inspiration, we call him by the noble name of artist.

That Mr. Booth was a man of genius in the vital conception, and a consummate artist in the varied expression of dramatic, and especially of Shakespearean character, we hope amply to illustrate, by a review of his more important personations, defined and refreshed by memoranda made at the time of their occurrence, during many years, for private reference and delight.

In person Mr. Booth was short, spare and muscular; with a head and face of antique beauty; dark hair; blue eyes; a neck and chest of ample but symmetrical mould; a step and movement elastic, assured, kingly. His face was pale, with that healthy pallor which is one sign of a magnetic brain. Throughout this brief, close-knit, imperial figure, Nature had planted or diffused her most vital organic forces; and made it the capable servant of the commanding mind that descended into and possessed it in every fibre.

The airy condensation of his temperament found fullest expression in his voice. Sound and capacious lungs, a vascular and fibrous throat, clearness and amplitude in the interior mouth and nasal passages, formed its physical basis. Words are weak, but the truth of those we shall employ, in an endeavor to suggest that voice, will be felt by multitudes who have been thrilled by its living tones. Deep, massive, resonant, many-stringed, changeful, vast in volume, of marvelous flexibility and range; delivering with ease, and power of instant and total interchange, trumpet-tones, bell-tones, tones like the "sound of many waters," like the muffled and confluent "roar of bleak-grown pines."

But no analogies in art or nature, and especially no indication of its organic structure and physical conditions, could reveal the inner secret of its charm. This charm lay in the mind, of which his voice was the organ: a "most miraculous organ," under the sway of a thoroughly informing mind. The chest voice became a fountain of passion and emotion. The head register gave the "clear, silver, icy, keen, awakening tones" of the pure intellect. And as the imagination stands, with its beautiful and comforting face, between heart and brain, and marries them with a benediction, giving glow to the thoughts, and form to the emotions, so there arose in this intuitive actor a third element of voice, hard to define, but of a fusing, blending, kindling quality, which we may name the imaginative, which appeared now in some single word, now with the full diapason of tones in some memorable sentence, and which distinguished him as an incomparable speaker of the English tongue. That voice was guided by a method which defied the set rules of elocution. It transcended music. It "brought airs from heaven and blasts from hell." It struggled and smothered in the pent fires of passion, or darted from them as in tongues of flame. It was "the earthquake voice of victory." It was, on occasion, full of tears and heart-break. Free as a fountain, it took the form and pressure of the conduit thought; and expressive beyond known parallel in voice of man, it suggested more than it expressed.

But his voice was marked by one significant limitation. It had no mirth. There were tones of light, but none of levity. No laughter, but that terrific laughter in Shylock, which seemed torn from his malignant heart at the announcement of Antonio's losses. It is true Mr. Booth played in farce. We have seen him repeatedly as Jerry Sneak, in Foote's farce of the "Mayor of Garratt;" and as Geoffry Muffincap, in "Amateurs and Actors." But his acting in this kind was never to our taste. It was not fun alive. His farce was simply the negation of his tragedy. In it he took the one step *from* the sublime. The sunny blue eye, the genial smile, the pleasantry we found so winning in social intercourse, never appeared upon the stage. His genius, and the voice it swayed, were dedicated to tragedy. Child of nature as he was, though consummated by art, he disdained no resource which might minister to the legitimate effects of tragedy. And it may be said that, as Phidias blended the lion into the god, in the face of his Jupiter, so Booth lifted the lion's voice, "the prowling lion's 'Here I am,'" into the human scale, and with judicious reserve and translated meaning bade it "roar and thunder in the index" of the stormier passions.

Such a man, so minded and so organized, we will not say justifies, he *necessitates* the stage. The moral argument is absorbed in the inevitable fact. If the theatre had not existed, he would have created it, according to the Divine order, in which the soul invents the circumstance. Without it, there would have been no field for the exercise of his peculiar powers. In him grand passions found play through the imagination, not only harmless, but fruitful and beautiful as art. Nay, it would seem as if the nature of this man lay, a distinct personality, embryonic in the very mind of Shakespeare, whose grander characters awaited, as the centuries rolled by, their destined and completed representative. And he came, in the fullness of time, to give them living form, and vital motion, and transcendant speech, and personal unity, and ever-endeared remembrance.

We must regard him as the greatest of all actors. Two names alone in the history of the stage, might dispute his supremacy — David Garrick and Edmund Kean. Garrick is a tradition. The record of his histrionic power is meagre. He seems to have been hampered by conventionalism, enacting Macbeth in a tie-wig and knee-breeches. His look is praised; and the power of his voice is illustrated by declamatory passages. No satisfactory analysis of his method has reached us. The anecdote that Dr. Johnson was overwhelmed by the pathos of his performance in Lear, is the most noteworthy circumstance of his life upon the stage. But Garrick played Tate's perversion, not Shakespeare's drama; and Johnson's morbid sensibility is well known.

Garrick was of French descent, and he seems to have inherited the vivacity, the point, the versatility, of the Gallic branch of the Celtic race. He was playwright, player, dancer, and a facile writer of epilogues and epigrams. He adapted, that is, altered for the stage, Cymbeline, Winter's Tale, Katherine and Petruchio. Dr. Johnson said that "his death eclipsed the gayety of nations." He was best in comedy, and his comic parts far outnumber the tragic. From all sources of knowledge on the subject, not omitting Fitzgerald's fascinating "Life of Garrick," recently published in London, we must conclude that his tragic acting, although a rare entertainment, did not touch the deepest springs of feeling; that it was rather a skill than an inspiration.

The inadequacy of Johnson's commentaries, stamps him, with all his vigorous English sense, as singularly deficient in the very quality which made Shakespeare the greatest of all dramatists, and which, whether in actor or critic, must be employed in interpreting his pages — we mean the quality of imagination. And we are without all evidence that the player went beyond the critic. That Garrick did not play up to the height of Shakespeare, is finally evident from the fact that Shakespeare himself was not truly known till a later day. Coleridge discovered him. Then Schlegel and other German thinkers (if indeed they did not precede Coleridge), caught his light, —

> "The light that never was on sea or lana,
> The consecration and the poet's dream,"

and reflected it back upon the English mind.

About this time Booth appeared, at the age of twenty, at Covent Garden Theatre, London. At another theatre, another actor of original force and fiery temperament, in the full maturity of his power and fame, the despot of the stage, jealous of all rivalry, was enacting Shakespeare to the wonder and admiration of the city; while such men as Coleridge, and Hazlitt, and Lamb, and Godwin, sat attentive in the pit. This actor was Edmund Kean.

"Two stars keep not their motion in one sphere." It is from the purpose of this essay to detail the circumstances of the war which followed, between the rival players. The curiosity of the reader may find satisfaction by looking into any authentic record of the English stage. What we have to do, is, briefly to note the respective forms of histrionic power in Kean and Booth; to trace these forms to their true sources in bodily and mental constitution, and to assign the superiority to whom it rightfully belongs.

There was a striking resemblance between

these two actors, in height and figure. In temperament, also, there was a partial similarity — both being distinguished by passionate energy, and by daring to displace the prescriptive habits of the stage, by the action and the tones of nature. To the English mind, observant of externals, and thrice-sodden in its regard for precedent, this superficial likeness, coupled with the mere fact that Booth was the younger and later product, seems to have suggested that he formed his style upon the acting of Kean. Nothing could be farther from the truth. We propose to state the points of difference between them, condensed from the widest range of the most unimpeachable testimony.

In Booth, the passionate energy, common to both, was sustained and expanded by a certain ethereal quality, wanting in Kean. Kean was alert; Booth, airy. Kean was black-eyed, like the children of Southern Europe. Booth had the blue eyes of the North,

> "Whence those arts and races sprung
> Which light, and lift, and sway the world."

The confined intensity of temperament in Kean, limited the range of his voice. Hazlitt speaks of him as having "the eye of an eagle, and the voice of a raven;" and elsewhere, while justly lauding the fire, the nature, the genius of his favorite, confesses to his "inharmonious voice." The voice obeys the emotion which dominates and employs it, and the pathos of Kean's utterance, particularly in certain passages of Othello, has probably never been surpassed.

In that admirable paper on the "Acting of Kean," written by Mr. Dana (himself a poet and imaginative critic of a high and delicate order of genius; and which brief record has gone far to continue the visionary and vanishing fame of the actor), he says, the pronunciation of the single word "Ha!" in Othello, when the feeling of jealousy is first awakened in his heart, seemed to carry away the listener "on its wild swell." Kean's throat was a cave of magical whispers. But, whether owing or not to the national catarrh, which afflicts the majority of Englishmen, and the influence of which upon the pronunciation of their native tongue is imitated by some absurd Americans, his voice was equally deficient in the ringing head tones, and in that resonant bass, not guttural, but far deeper, which Booth used with such masculine and memorable effect. We find accordingly in Kean's voice a peculiarity, a mannerism, in which the liquids *m* and *n* had no place, but which consisted in a prolongation of the liquids *l* and *r*.

"Farewell-l-l the pl-l-lumèd trrroop."

The most cordial tribute to Kean's excellence, was given us by one who, by the law of retaliation, was under the least obligation to render it, namely, by Mr. Booth himself. Similar magnanimity Kean never would have shown. But Mr. Booth, throughout a changeful career, marked by human infirmity, and running sometimes on the giddy verge of madness, was always a gentleman as well as a scholar; while it must be owned that Kean, great as were his histrionic claims, was neither the one nor the other.

There existed however a distinction, more radical than temperament, or education, or manners, which separated these two actors, and lay in the very core of the mental life of each. Look at the portraits of Kean. All concur (even that one with the Kemble eyebrow, which Kean had not) in giving him a brain wide at the base, pinched at the temples; in marked contrast with the winged and balanced brain of Booth. Correspondingly, all records and all reports agree, in representing Kean's performances as fearfully intense, inevitable, aiming to express character by single strokes of overwhelming energy, or heart-broken pathos; and leaving between the strokes wide intervals of dullness.

Coleridge said that to see him act, "was like reading Shakespeare by flashes of lightning." John Kemble said, "the little fellow is terribly in earnest." All records agree — all but one. Macaulay, in his "History of England," in one of those brief and brilliant episodes which beguile the progress of the story, traces the pedigree of Kean to the Marquis of Halifax — through how many escapades of illegitimacy he does not confess. He says, the Marquis was the progenitor of "that Edmund Kean, who, in our own time, transformed himself so marvelously into Shylock, Iago, and Othello." If this be true, no higher praise could be awarded to any actor. If this be true, then the portraits, and Kemble, and Hazlitt, and Coleridge, and a multitude of contemporary observers now living, are all at fault.

We think it will require something more than the dazzling dogmatism of the English historian, to sustain his position. We think, not that Kean transformed himself into Shylock, Iago, and Othello; but that the actor transformed those characters respectively into Edmund Kean: that is, that he took just those words, and lines, and points, and passages, in the character he was to represent, which he found suited to his genius, and gave them with electric force. His method was limitary. It was analytic and passionate; not, in the highest sense, intellectual and imaginative.

Our final authority is Hazlitt, who has given, in his work on the "English Stage," by far the most thorough exposition of Kean's powers. Hazlitt learnt him by heart. He delved him to the root, and let in on his merits and defects the irradiating and the "insolent light" of a searching criticism. He says, with fine hyperbole, that to see Kean at his best, in Othello, "was one of the consolations of the human mind;" yet is constrained to admit, even in his notice of this play, that "Kean lacked — imagination."

Now this power Booth possessed of a subtile kind, and in magnificent measure. It lent a weird expressiveness to his voice. It atmosphered his most terrific performances with beauty. Booth took up Kean at his best, and carried him further. Booth was Kean, *plus* the higher imagination. Kean was the intense individual; Booth, the type *in* the intense individual. To see Booth in his best mood was *not* "like reading Shakespeare by flashes of lightning," in which a blinding glare alternates with the fearful suspense of darkness; but rather like reading him by the sunlight of a summer's day, a light which casts deep shadows, gives play to glorious harmonies of color, and shows all objects in vivid life and true relation.

The recorded impression left by Kean on the minds of his reporters and biographers, is of a mighty grasp and overwhelming energy in partial scenes; while Booth is remembered for his sustained and all-related conception of character, intensely realized, it is true, but chiefly marked by those ideal traits, which not only charmed the listener, but accompanied the scholar to his study, and shed a light on the subtlest and the profoundest page of Shakespeare. The imaginative power was so opulent in Booth, that he multiplied himself into the scene, and abolished the dullness of the other players. Filled with the conception of the supernatural himself, he "shook the superflux to them." In Hamlet, he made the tread and exit of the heaviest "ghost," airier; and in Macbeth, transformed by his presence and action, the three fantastic old women into ministers of fate.

In according to Booth the gift of supreme histrionic power, we do not imply that his performances were faultless; for the faultless performer is simply the correct. We willingly admit that he may have been matched by others, and haply surpassed in all secondary qualities, excepting voice, which illuminate the stage; he holding, beyond rivalry, the single controlling quality of a penetrating, kindling, shaping imagination. Genius can light its own fire; and it is the peculiar property of histrionic genius to cherish, manipulate, and apply the flame. Yet in the finest results of all art there is something independent of the will. *Mr. Booth was perhaps the most unequal of all great actors.* And this inequality was more sadly manifest towards the latter part of his career. His excellence was, however, throughout his life, so incalculable and surprising, that one of his very greatest Shakespearean performances took place in the year 1850, during his last engagement in Boston.

Health, animal spirits, that vigor which comes from just intervals of repose, clearness of voice in our trying climate, and general freshness of the physical man, may all conspire to serve the exacting hour, and yet the spontaneous actor not find himself "i' the vein." The transforming imaginative power on which he relies to identify himself with the dramatic character, may be either sluggish or asleep. The whence and whither of that wind of the spirit, who knoweth? So Mr. Booth, to the casual attendant on his performances, often failed to sustain his great reputation. Only to those who, like ourselves, had waited on them through remunerating years, did the full depth and refinement, the glow and sway of mind he showed, entirely appear. Many a time, when passion and imagination were comparatively wanting, have we admired the subtle intellect of his interpretations; and were, on such occasions, content to follow his lifted and guiding torch, along the spar-gemmed labyrinths of Shakespeare's more intricate meanings.

Our course of remark has drifted us into that cloud which hung over and partially obscured his fame, and which, in good men's minds, affixed a blot on his personal character. We mean what has been called, with needless exaggeration, his habit of intoxication. We would gladly avoid this subject, but "omittance is no quittance," and we proceed to set the charge in its true light. During the forty years, save one, which bounded his dramatic career, Mr. Booth's *habit* of life, both on his farm and on the stage, was exemplarily temperate. His reverence for the sacredness of all life amounted to a superstition. He abstained for many years on principle from the use of animal food. An "extravagant and erring spirit," allied to madness, would sometimes take possession of him, and hurry him away from the theatre at the moment the performance was to begin; and to this cause, and not to intoxication, should be attributed the not infrequent disappointment of the audience. Still it must be confessed, with grief and pity, that the baser charge was often true. A resort to stimulants is the actor's special bane and ever-present temptation: to an actor of Mr. Booth's spontaneous method, sometimes an irresistible temptation. The histrionic art was to him a *cultus*, a religion. Not to speak it profanely, he offered himself a perpetual sacrifice to the god of terror and of beauty; he staked "soul and body on the action both," and the exhaustion sometimes attendant upon *his* performance of the fiery rite, was relieved by means questionable, pitiful, pardonable.

The accident by which his nose was broken, spoiling forever his noble profile, threatened for a time the more serious disaster of a permanent injury to his voice. Immediately on his recovery he began to play. To those who, during these first performances, recalled the perfect features and the resonant tones of former years, the sight and sound were indeed pitiful. The head tones were scarcely perceptible. But instead of humoring this vocal infirmity, he spoke with all the old mastery of motive, and let the result take care of itself. By this persistent method, in less than two years after the accident, his voice had completely recovered its original scope, variety, and power; as we can attest by close, solicitous, and comparative observation. To this restoration, added to the autumnal ripeness of his physical and mental powers, we owe the undiminished zest and life of his impersonations.

We pass on to examples, in the hope that the reader will bring to our record that "productive imagination" which alone can render fruitful the endeavor to rekindle the fire of eye and action, to give form to air, to bring a voice out of the silent past, and to conjure up before him a kingly and inspiring presence.

RICHARD III.

We do not quarrel with Colley Cibber, player and playwright of the time of Garrick, because he saw fit, for the convenience of the stage, to compose, out of several historical plays of Shakespeare, in which the same characters occur, one entitled "Richard the Third." But we do blame him for his audacious excision of the living limbs, his more audacious interpolations in the text, and his senseless changes in the character of that Richard, third of the name, whom Shakespeare delineated. He has obliterated those lights of human feeling, which the great master touched in, and which alone redeem Richard from the condition of vulgar villainy, into which Cibber plunges him. The buoyant, aspiring soul of the usurper, finding expression in such language as this —

> "But I was born so high,
> Our aiery buildeth in the cedar's top
> And dallies with the wind, and scorns the sun,"

does nowhere appear.

In Shakespeare, the villainy is incidental to the ambition; and is besides relieved by genius, energy, and vast and ready variety of intellectual resources. In Cibber's version, villainy is the substance of the character; the very element in which it sits and revels. In Shakespeare, when multiplying dangers and ghostly visitation have combined to open in Richard's soul "the access and passage to remorse," occurs this remarkable utterance: —

> "There is no creature loves me,
> And if I die no soul will pity me!"

Cibber wantonly hardens the depravity of the character, below its all-sufficient wickedness. The interpolated scene with Lady Anne, whom Richard had widowed, cajoled, married, and resolved to slay, is simply atrocious and inhuman.

But the play, such as it is, shining with Shakespeare's genius, blotted by Cibber's folly, has always held the stage; and it is less our purpose to complain of its defects, than to show Mr. Booth's masterly impersonation of the leading part. He is identified with it in the public mind. His performance of it was certain, at any period of his life, to crowd the theatre. And in truth, although it excluded all opportunity for the display of the finer traits of his genius, yet the energy, subtlety, variety, he brought to its representation — the sustained vigor of voice, and look, and action, to the last — justified the popular approval.

In Mr. Booth's conception the main impulse was most apparent; the ambition, and not the crimes it caused. There was a certain slow movement at the opening; a sombre settled purpose, underlying and surrounding his most brilliant action; and giving place at last to a preternatural energy, and fiery expedition, only when the object, the crown, was attained, and all the resources of his fertile brain were drawn on and combined, in the effort to retain the regal power he had usurped.

With head bent in thought, arms folded, and slow long step, longer it would seem than the height of his figure might warrant, yet perfectly natural to him, and so that his lifted foot emerged first into view, Booth appeared upon the scene, enveloped and absorbed in the character of Richard.

If tumultuous plaudits extorted from him

a momentary recognition of the audience, it was done with no suspension of the look and action of the character. That look and action were profoundly self-involved. He delivered the soliloquy beginning —

"Now is the winter of our discontent,"

in an inward many-stringed resonance of tone, varied by outbursts of passionate vehemence, when "descanting on his own deformity," and reaching through murderous intent after the glorious diadem. He spoke like a man thinking aloud, not as if reciting from memory. Indeed, to speak with strictness, he never re-cited at all. He possessed himself of the character, and its language, and then uttered it from inspiration, and according to the emergency of the scene and the situation. Memory, the prime need of an actor, speedily becomes his greatest danger; a danger lurking always in repetitions of performance, but one into which our actor seldom if ever fell. He carried distinctness of articulation to an extreme, pronouncing "ocean," in this soliloquy, as a word of three syllables.

In the sequent scene where Gloster having killed King Henry, exclaims with bitter scorn —

"What! Will the aspiring blood of Lancaster
Sink in the ground? I thought it would have mounted!"

he lifts his sword, and his eye following, catches sight of blood upon the blade, in a manner like the very truth of nature. He adds —

"See! How my sword weeps for the poor king's death!
O! may such *purple* tears be always shed,
By those who wish the downfall of our house."

What grim humor was in that cold, self-poised recollection, contained in the words —

"Indeed, 'tis true, that Henry told me of,"

Henry lying then warm but dead by his hand, and alone with him in the kingly bed-chamber!

Originality in Mr. Booth's performances was a necessity of his genius. His acting was a congeries of causes, coördinated with the main cause, the conception of the character. Kean's manner of acting, on the contrary, was a series of disconnected brilliant effects. Gloster's wooing scene with Lady Anne is a case in point.

The best character portrait of Kean, represents him on one knee, smiling, and saying —

"Take up the sword again, or take up me."

Hazlitt says, "The whole scene was an admirable exhibition of smooth and smiling villainy." Booth made no such exhibition. He did not kneel gracefully. The question with him was not, how is courtship done; but how would Gloster do it. Nothing would be more likely to charm so weak a woman as Lady Anne, than the repentance and humility of so powerful a nature as that of Richard. "You may relish him more in the soldier than in the lover." Personal flattery was thrown in as a spice, and not as the substance of the dish he offered her. Surprise was blent with joy at his hoped-for victory, in the glance he darted up from his abasement at her feet, when Lady Anne drops the sword. Surprise which finds vent in words, as soon as he finds himself alone.

"Was ever woman in this humor wooed?
Was ever woman in this humor *won?*
I'll have her — but I will not keep her long."

The whole soliloquy was given with that massive, vivid, and varied intonation, which might express the tumult of feelings awakened by his almost incredible success. How fine the sudden halt, in that repeated descant on his own deformity, and airy change of tone, in the passage beginning —

> "My dukedom to a beggarly denier
> I do mistake my person all this while."

Nothing could exceed the picturesque beauty of his action, as he delivered the closing lines —

> "Shine out fair sun, till I salute my glass,
> That I may see my shadow as I pass."

He looked down at his supposed shadow (we seem to see the shadow as we write); he looked with lingering step, and, with pauses between the words, annihilated the sing-song of the double ending —

> "That I may see — my shadow — as — I pass."

The flexible grasp with which Mr. Booth laid hold of and personated the elements of a character, permitted certain minor variations, both in by-play and intonation, in different performances of the same part, without injuring, but rather heightening, the general effect. This freshened the interest in successive exhibitions, and gave scope oftentimes to rare and vanishing delicacies of thought and feeling. An instance occurred in the scene between Gloster and the young prince Edward, sometimes given thus: —

Gloster (*aside*). "So wise, so young (they say), do ne'er live long," as if musing complacently on the proverb, yet scarcely harboring the purpose of making it true. And again thus: —

"So wise, so young, *they say*, do ne'er live long."

as if the proverb was but the cloak of his full-blown intent to "remove" the prince.

From this point he developed the character with ever-increasing animation and momentum. His change of manner when seated on the throne was marked and majestic, and in fine contrast with the wily, plotting approaches to it. Buckingham, the agent of his elevation, stands at once and forever in the shadow of his kingly will. Booth's tone and action acquired a combined solidity and celerity, which continued, with brief but fearful interruptions in the latter scenes, to the end of the play.

We may here note an apparent error in his manner of replying to Buckingham's urgent and reiterated demand for the promised earldom. He says: —

"Thou troublest me. I'm *not* i' the vein,"

in a tone of fretful anger. The passage would seem rather to require a tone of cool and kingly slight. Shakespeare amplifies the retort, and has this line, left out in Cibber's version: —

"I am not in the *giving* vein to-day."

In the scene where Richard pleads with Queen Elizabeth for her daughter's hand, and says —

"When this warlike arm shall have chastised
The audacious rebel, hot-brained Buckingham,
Bound with triumphant garlands will I come,
And lead your daughter to a conqueror's bed,"

we cannot express the splendor of his manner better than by saying, that it suggested the majestic march, the mighty music, and the flower-like play of color of a Roman triumph. Lord Stanley enters with these words: —

'Richmond is on the seas."

Richard. "There let him *sink*" (*plummet*), "*and be the seas on him*" (like the lift, advance, and fall of one huge whelming wave), "white-livered runagate" (between set teeth, like hissing foam).

In this dialogue with Stanley, Booth restored a passage from Shakespeare, not in Cibber's play, but essential to the character of Richard, who, fighting to maintain his throne, seems really to feel himself "the Lord's anointed." In reply to Stanley's suggestion that Richmond came to claim the crown, Richard bursts forth —

"Is the chair empty? Is the sword unswayed? Is the king dead?"

The solid, smiting questions, the momentary pause between, as rendered by Booth, can never be forgotten by those who heard them. The questions continue and culminate in that memorable passage —

> "What do they i' the North,
> When they should serve their sovereign i' the West?"

The last line was delivered in one continuous tone of commanding resonance, in which the words were dropped like stones in the current of his speech.

In the concluding scenes of this play he seemed, when in his best mood, to be filled with "strange fire." He showed infinite vigilance of mind, relentless mastery of will. The tent scene, in which Richard starts out of his remorseful dream, was one of terrific grandeur, and never failed of producing an electrical effect. After he had mastered the harrowing thoughts born of his dream, his utterance of the words —

> "Richard's himself again,"

constituted a brief but pointed study of character. A distinguished tragedian, now living and performing, and therefore here unnamed, could find no better gesture for Richard's self-recovery than to strike a fencing attitude.

But Booth stood still, and with one inclusive, unanalyzable motion of the hand, took limbs, body, heart, and brain, in its subtle and commanding sweep, while he delivered the passage expressing his inward victory with inward voice —

> "As if a man were author of himself
> And knew no other kin!"

In the following scene, when Stanley's defection is announced, Richard exclaims —

> "Off with his son George's head."

At that moment his ear catches the sound of distant music, and his whole manner instantly changes. He listens, leaning on the air with keen looks and parted lips, and an expression of eager and confident expectation.

> *Norfolk.* "My lord, the foe's already past the marsh;
> After the battle let young Stanley die."
> *Richard.* "Why, after be it then."

He said this in a tone of the lightest and most careless readiness, still listening; then resumed his energy of manner in the brief and stirring appeal to his soldiers, as he led them into the fight.

In the last scene he fought with Richmond desperately; when wounded and overthrown, fought on the ground. Finally, gathering himself up with one mighty effort, he plunged headlong at his cool antagonist, was disarmed, and felled to the earth. Cibber has put into the mouth of the dying Richard, some wretched and inhuman stuff, which, to the credit of Mr. Booth be it said, we could never distinctly hear from his lips. It sounded only like —

> "The cloudy groan
> Of dying thunder on the distant wind."

HAMLET.

The character of Hamlet has been, ever since the time of Shakespeare, the delight and the puzzle of scholars. The portrayal of it has been equally the ambition and the failure of actors. The scholar finds the drama eminently a tragedy of thought, and is apt to refine into abstraction the personality of the hero. The actor, depending in his art on presence and speech, usually fails to sound the depth of the character, to pluck out the heart of its mystery, and so gives its varied incident, action, dialogue, soliloquy, in a succession of incoherent, perhaps brilliant, effects.

In Mr. Booth's conception, Hamlet was a character, not of melancholy, but of a predominant sensibility, which included melancholy. Not of madness, but of one who, bound by strange ties to the invisible world, found his large discourse of reason and his mastery of will *distracted* between opposing duties. In Hamlet, filial love amounted to a passion. And his father's spirit, in arms, appeared visibly to him, and audibly commanded him, in terms of solemn adjuration, to commit a deed abhorrent to his feelings as a man. Booth's Hamlet was intensely personal. His brain was —

> "The quick forge and working-house of thought."

His heart was full of purpose, as of affection. His indecision was the result of circumstances, not a defect of will. But this positive and personal life was so atmosphered by beauty, so steeped in melancholy, so spiritualized by supernatural emotion, that it seemed to us, in all essential qualities, the very Hamlet of Shakespeare.

That phase of this many-sided creation to which he gave least effect, was the princeliness. That pensive grace and high breeding which many regard as Hamlet's permanent condition, ruffled only by passing gusts of passion, illuminated by fitful lights of philosophy and fancy, and crazed by ghostly visitation, — found in him an indifferent interpreter. He seemed too severely exercised by "thoughts beyond the reaches of his soul" to mind the graces of the court; and his manner was seldom gentle, but rather "swift as meditation." Hamlet was Booth's favorite part.

Among unnumbered representations, we select for special comment one which took place at the Howard Athenæum, in Boston, on that very winter's night when the steamer Atlantic was lost upon Long Island Sound, in a furious snow-storm —

> "A brave vessel
> Which had no doubt some noble creatures in her,
> Dashed all to pieces."

Owing to the weather the attendance was small. This circumstance aided the illusion of the opening scene, as if the scattered spectators were accidentally present, and looking at the chilled and lonely sentinels, pacing the ramparts of Elsinore castle. But the audience was fit though few. An eminent Shakespearean scholar sat with us, and a knot of literary friends. It was a noteworthy fact, however it might be accounted for, that Mr. Booth seemed to play better to a thin house.

He appeared on the stage with his features marred, with his natural hair turned iron-gray, and with no special help from costume, or scenery, or the other actors. But never did the soul of Hamlet shine forth more clearly with its own peculiar, fitful, far-reaching, saddened, and supernatural light.

He was not merely sad, but stricken in grief, at the sudden and mysterious death of his father. He is stung by instinctive suspicion of his uncle. He is shamed and outraged by his mother's hasty and incestuous marriage. He sobs audibly. When his "uncle father" addresses him —

> "But now my cousin Hamlet, and my son,"

he answers aside, in bitter murmur —

> "A little more than kin, and less than kind."

To his mother's vague generalization about the commonness of death, he answers with restrained respect —

> "Ay, madam, it *is* — common."

But when she urges a question of cold complaint, he vindicates the profound sincerity of his grief, in that fine speech beginning —

> "Seems, madam! nay, it is."

We pause upon this passage, for in the searching and thoughtful emphasis he gave to its delivery, Mr. Booth struck the key-note of Hamlet's character, the depth of which neither action nor language, however eloquent or effective, could ever fully reveal. "He had that *within* which passeth show."

Hamlet is left alone, and instantly unburdens his heart in the soliloquy beginning —

> "O, that this too, too solid flesh would melt."

Did Shakespeare intend the speech to be uttered aloud, or only mused upon? The question becomes pertinent, in view of Lamb's objection to the stage representation of the play, where he speaks of Hamlet's "light-and-noise-abhorring ruminations." We think the terse vigor of the language would find a tongue. It did find an eloquent tongue in our actor. The jostle of thoughts, the impatient leaps of emotion, all crowding for utterance, found meet expression in his rapid and changeful delivery.

> "Frailty, thy *name* is woman,"

as if no other name were needed.

> "Married with mine uncle (*pause*),
> My father's brother" (*in low and slighting tones*),

then without pause —

> "But no more *like my father*
> Than I to Hercules."

The following scene is chiefly remarkable

for the report to Hamlet of the appearance of the ghost. How fit that this disclosure should be made by Horatio, whose gracious, limited, and firm-seated nature becomes, from this moment, coolness to the fever, and counterpoise to the perturbation of his princely friend, even to the closing scene of the play, when Hamlet lies dead in his arms! The spiritual tone Booth imparted to this scene, weighted as it is by specific questions and answers, as to the time and aspect of the apparition, raised the listener at once into the rare atmosphere of Hamlet's being, and culminated in this remarkable soliloquy: —

> "My father's spirit — *in arms!* All is not well;
> I doubt some foul play: would the night were come!
> Till then sit still, my soul: foul deeds will rise,
> Though all the earth o'erwhelm them, to men's eyes."

Booth uttered the words, "Foul deeds will rise," as with the voice of Fate. Then came the mighty parenthesis, "Though all the earth o'erwhelm them," which he gave with a sweeping gesture, as if taking the solid earth, and lifting it as a wave of the sea is lifted, and letting it fall. He then raised a warning hand, with significant motion, before his face, and with changed voice, couching strength of emphasis on a lower range of tones, resumed the suspended meaning—"to men's eyes."

In the platform scene, his adjuration of the Spirit reached a climax of feeling in the word "father," into which he threw the agony of his grief, and the contending hope and fear born of this strange visitation. After a momentary pause, the figure remaining silent, Hamlet recommences, and delivers without pause the following:—

> "Royal Dane, O, answer me."

In all editions of the play, there is a colon after "Royal Dane." Booth overruled this pause, with a more subtle perception of the meaning of the passage than has been shown by any commentator.

The first effect of the sudden apparition passes rapidly off; and Hamlet soon finds himself in strange and calm accord with the silent but beckoning visitor. To the dissuasion of his friends he says:—

> "Why, what should be the fear?
> I do not set my life at a pin's fee,
> And for my soul, what can it do to that,
> Being a thing immortal—as itself?"

Booth's manner here is hard to analyze. It

may suffice to say, that both tone and action scaled the heights of spiritual thought. He seemed to have digested in his soul the very bitterness of death, to have passed beyond, and to speak as one conscious of his immortality. In fine contrast came the passionate outbreak —

> "My fate cries out
> And makes each petty artery in this body
> As hardy as the Nemean lion's nerve."

We know not whether the action originated with Mr. Booth or not: but in the scene following the terrible revelation of the Spirit, when his friends find him, and he swears them to secrecy, Hamlet holds up the hilt of his sword, the cross, and not the blade, for the imposition of their hands. We have seen, both in picture and on the stage, the hands of Horatio and Marcellus laid along the blade. In this scene, the "antic disposition," which has so puzzled critic and actor, begins to play. In Booth's conception, this was partly a reaction from the pressure of supernatural emotion; and partly assumed as a disguise. Its fitful light seemed native to the genius of our actor. It gave variety and unexpectedness in look, and tone, and action, throughout the play. It shone above the melancholy, like phosphorescence on a midnight sea, with most intensifying effect. The scenes with Polonius, where Hamlet plays upon him ; the scenes with his school-fellows, in which he shows he cannot be played upon ; and the scenes with the players, are instances in point.

> *Ghost* (*beneath*). Swear.
> *Hamlet.* There are more things in heaven and *earth*, Horatio,
> Than are dreamt of in your *philosophy*."

A light scorn in the last word : and his hand passed his forehead, with a gesture equally light and evanescent.

Perhaps the most brilliant example of that *unexpectedness* which is genius in an actor, as if he indeed were the character assumed ; as if the thoughts were developed from within, and the language *occurred* to him, might be found in the passage beginning —

> "I have of late (but wherefore I know not) lost all my mirth."

At the words, "This most excellent canopy, the air, look you, — this brave o'erhanging" (he omitted the word "firmament," as in the folio), "this majestical roof fretted with golden fire," — his voice, sombre and husky in the preceding lines, suddenly darted upward like light; seemed to penetrate the sky; to run all over the firmament; to search out and give back the remotest echoes of heaven. The speaker was for the moment forgot, —

> "Hidden
> In the light of thought."

"He that plays the king shall be welcome," was uttered with eager emphasis, a momentary betrayal by Hamlet of his inner thought; which however he masks immediately, by a running and cheery commentary on the other players. Hamlet has received, seen through, talked with, and dismissed his school-mates; puzzled Polonius by subtle reaches of wit; welcomed the players with a volatile and princely grace; shown a combined freedom and aptitude in all this surface-play of mind, this "whiff and wind" of thought, over the deep sea of his sad spirit, — most wonderful in Shakespeare, and reproduced by Booth as in a mirror; until he finds himself alone, when he reveals his latent purpose in that soliloquy in which the lines occur: —

> "I'll have these players
> Play something like the murder of my father
> Before mine uncle."

and closing with —

> "The play 's the thing
> Wherein I'll catch the conscience of the king."

Our Shakespearean scholar found fault with an emphasis, after the act was done. "Booth emphasized 'catch,'" said he; "he should have emphasized 'conscience.'" Not so. The actor's spontaneous method gave life to the whole passage. He really emphasized *both* words, and all in due relation. The Third Act opened. The play went on. The atmosphere of Hamlet, with whose very being Booth was for the time consubstantiated, enveloped also the listening scholar, and gradually nourished him out of his meagre mood of verbal criticism. And to that degree did the influence work, that we heard him uttering unconscious groans for sympathy, as the catastrophe drew near and that foreboding illness, "here about the heart," found expression in tones of mournful, tender trust: —

> "If it be now, 'tis not to come. If it be not now, yet it will come: the readiness is all. Let be."

Hamlet repeatedly revolves the problem of suicide. We have seen that he does not "set his life at a pin's fee;" but his conscience, the very strength of his moral nature, which withholds his hand from attempting his own life, also makes him fear to take that of the king. The beginning of the meditation "To be, or not to be" was uttered in a voice like the mystic murmur of a river running under ground, and required an attentive ear: "That undiscovered country" (in a manner unimaginably remote) "from whose bourn no traveller *returns*" — given with accelerated and vibrating intensity, the stroke of emphasis coming suprisingly on the last word. It shocked the elocutionist, but delighted the Shakespearean scholar.

The soliloquy was marked by a curious reading, thus: —

> "For who would bear the whips and scorns of time,
>
> . . . .
>
> When he himself might his quietus make."

Here he made a full stop. Then, as if beginning a new sentence, and without pause in the delivery of it, he went on —

> "With a bare bodkin who would fardels bear, etc.

On being called to account for this odd reading, he affirmed, that " bodkin " was a local term, in some parts of England, for a padded yoke, worn over the shoulders for the support of burdens on either side ; and that a " *bare* bodkin " was a yoke without the pad, and therefore galling. The meaning assigned, has, we believe, escaped the notice of all lexicographers.

On suddenly discovering Ophelia — his meditation done — with what tremulous tenderness did he say —

> " Nymph, in thy orisons
> Be all my sins remembered."

In the acting play, Hamlet is made to catch a glimpse of the king and his minister at espial: the discovery being intended to account for his harshness towards Ophelia. We find no warrant for this in Shakespeare. The intuitive Hamlet knows, it is true, by Ophelia's manner, that she is acting a part under instructions. But we think every one of his speeches to her is justified by his own nature; by his assumed madness; or by his endeavor to wipe away both from his own mind and hers, " all trivial fond records," so that the commandment of the Spirit " all alone may live " —

"Within the book and volume of his brain" —

and all without supposing him to be aware of other listeners.

In spite of the set purpose, his deep love bursts forth in jets of passionate tenderness. It did so in Mr. Booth's rendering. He spoke with wildness rather than severity. He was in constant action; striding across the stage; passing out, still speaking, and beginning the next speech before he reëntered. We seem now to hear his voice ringing, out of view, the phrase —

"I have heard of your paintings too, well enough."

Only when imploring her to go to a nunnery did he pause in action; then, approaching her tenderly, he threw into those oft-repeated words "to a nunnery, go," the whole force of his fervent affection.

Mr. Macready played Hamlet in Boston, and Cambridge crowded the boxes — yes, and applauded too, as that sensible but unimaginative actor gave his studied version of Hamlet's idleness.

Hamlet (to Horatio). "They are coming to the play; I must be idle:
Get you a place."

Macready seemed unaccountably to have

changed natures with Osric the "waterfly;" for he danced before the foot-lights, flirting a white handkerchief above his head! This was that "famed performer" to whom Emerson refers, when he says: "All I then heard, and all I now remember, of the tragedian, was that in which the tragedian had no part; simply, Hamlet's question to the ghost —

> 'What may this mean,
> That thou, dead corse, again in complete steel.
> Revisit'st thus the glimpses of the moon?'"

Booth's idleness was Hamlet's. He retires up the stage, passes from view, and reappears like a shadow; is lost in the company that enters to witness the play. We find him next at Ophelia's feet, at once Mercury and Nemesis, the lover's wit playing airily above the avenging purpose.

(We may here mention that in the year 1831, Mr. Booth became the temporary manager of a theatre in Baltimore. Mr. Charles Kean enacted Hamlet. Mr. Booth, on this occasion, assumed the part of Lucianus, called in the play-bills, "the second actor," whose whole office it is to say —

> "Thoughts black, hands apt, drugs fit, and time agreeing;
> Confederate season, else no creature seeing;

Thou mixture rank, of midnight weeds collected,
With Hecate's ban thrice blasted, thrice infected
Thy natural magic and dire property,
On wholesome life usurp immediately."

In Booth's delivery of these fearful lines, each word dropped poison. The weird music of his voice and the stealthy yet decisive action, made this brief scene the memorable event of the night.)

The king does blench "Upon the *talk* of the poisoning;" he rises "frighted with false fire." The play within the play abruptly ends. Hamlet is left alone. To him come, first his traitor school-fellows; then the meddling Polonius, envoys of the king and queen.

In two lines of the short soliloquy which follows, the tragedian indicated, by a master-stroke of intonation and expression, the span and sweep of Hamlet's nature: the restraining force of will, acting as counterpoise to the momentum of his feelings.

"Soft; now to my mother.
O heart, lose not thy nature; let not ever
The soul of Nero enter this firm bosom."

The thought of Nero's crime seemed suddenly to occur to him, to fill him with horror, and to lend to the word "Nero" a surprising repulsion of gesture and emphasis.

These lines were a fit prologue to the great scene of the play, in the Third Act, the interview with his mother. The strong current, the earnest pleading, the impassioned conscience, the noble purpose, the intense personal life, made manifest by Mr. Booth in this scene, might serve as a study for those, who, impressed by a single trait in this "abstract and brief chronicle" of civilized man — this Hamlet — weakly conclude him to be full of weakness, and of a melancholy born of weakness. His melancholy was born of his strength.

> "Mother, *you* have — *my father* — much offended."
>
> . . . .
>
> "Come, come, and sit you down; you shall not budge;
> You go not, till I set you up a glass
> Where you shall see the *in*-most part of you!"

He had already said —

> "I will *speak* — *daggers* to her."

That word "*inmost*" touched the core of the matter. The sound of it, greatly prolonged on the first syllable, was like a searching probe of steel. After he had killed Polonius, mistaking him for the king, he gave separately each word of the line —

"Thou wretched, rash, intruding fool, farewell!"

and all with ascending emphasis, in tones of mingled grief and anger, and as if dashed with tears.

What exalted passion is in the continuing portion of this scene! In the comparison of the portraits, what dramatic action, thought, imagery, language! We know this tribute belongs to Shakespeare. We make it, looking towards him, where he sits, in the glory and beatitude of his own peculiar heaven. All we claim for Mr. Booth, all that can be claimed for any actor, is, that he shall, by the power of imaginative sympathy, pass himself, and draw us after, into the strong current of Shakespeare's thought; shall remould and rekindle to our attentive senses, the individuality of his unmatched characters.

Looking on the picture of his father he says —

"Where *every* god, did seem to set his seal."

. . . .

"This — *was* — your husband" (*kissing the picture and in a voice that sheathed affection for his father, in reprobation for his mother*). "Look you now what follows" (*with startling change of manner*) —

> "Here is-s-s your husband, like a mildewed ear
> Blasting his wholesome brother!"

The words of this phrase were shaken and eddied over by one continuing flood of tone; in obedience to a passionate method, most expressive and quite peculiar to our actor.

At the opportune moment, when the heat of his indignation finds expression thus —

> "A murderer and a villain;
> . . . .
> A cutpurse of the empire and the rule,"

the ghost appears. There seemed to pass over Booth's features an instant baptism of devotion. All anger vanished. The outreaching and imploring look in his full blue eyes, arching the inner angles of the brows, gave the face a tender exaltation, as he began that strange colloquy between Hamlet, his guilty mother, and his father's spirit, with the words —

> "What would your gracious figure?"

During the presence of the ghost, until just before its exit at the opposite door, Booth stood rooted to the spot from which he first saw it; stood with steady gaze, outstretched hands, and such pathetic reverence of voice and action, that, though we looked and listened then in a mood above weeping, yet the memory of it surprises us, as we write, "unto the brink of tears."

Ghost. "Speak to her, Hamlet."
Ham. (*Still looking at the ghost.*) "How is it with you, lady?"
Queen. "Whereon do you look?"
Ham. "*On* him, *on* him" (*as if the question were idle; as if she must see the figure also*).

In the oft-quoted passage —

"Assume a virtue if you have it not,"

Booth paused after "virtue," then uttered the words, "if you have it not," as if a spring of love gushed in his heart, and he caught at a hope, that she *might* have repented already.

In the grave-yard scene, after he has matched wit with the clown, and given another example of that blended airiness and melancholy which seemed the very form of Shakespeare's thought, the funeral procession of Ophelia enters.

Hamlet (*to Horatio*). "That is Laertes,
A very noble youth: mark" —

uttered with perfect simplicity and generous high breeding. Perhaps in qualification of an opinion heretofore expressed, the princeliness came out more strongly in Mr. Booth's delineation of these later scenes. When Laertes says —

> "A ministering angel shall my sister be,"

Hamlet, according to the text, utters the exclamation —

> "What! the fair Ophelia!"

No syllable of this phrase could be heard. Only a wild, inarticulate cry escaped him; and he muffled his face in his cloak. He seemed to have gone behind Shakespeare's language, into Shakespeare's thought.

Following this fine touch of feeling and character, came what seems to us a wholly unauthorized reading: —

> "What is he whose grief
> Bears such an emphasis? whose phrase of sorrow
> Conjures the wandering stars, and bids them stand
> Like wonder-wounded hearers? This is I,
> Hamlet the Dane."

So Shakespeare; but Booth made a full stop after the word "stand;" then said —

> "Look! wonder-wounded hearers, this is I," etc.

The scene, however, was grandly carried to completion. The storm of mingled grief and love for the dead Ophelia; of anger breaking through respect, for Laertes, could never have had a more characteristic representation.

Hamlet consents to play the wager with Laertes, but is possessed by a presentiment of evil. We had heard Mr. Booth give the passage thus: —

> "It is but foolery, but it is such a kind of gain-giving as would, perhaps (*slight pause, then in lower tone*), trouble a *woman*,"

meaning, "it ought not to trouble me, a man, yet I feel it does." On this occasion he said —

> "As would, perhaps, *trouble* (*slight pause*) a *woman*,"

meaning, "but shall not trouble me." How fine the sentiment, how delicate the apprehension, that could dictate these distinctions. The wavering balance inclines toward the latter reading; for to Horatio's friendly dissuasion, Hamlet immediately rejoins —"Not a whit; we defy augury; there is a special providence in the fall of a sparrow." Rufus Choate said, "I have seen him act Hamlet exquisitely:" and again, in comparing Kean and Booth, he said, "This man (Booth) has finer touches."

The last scene was full of grace and dramatic truth, in the fencing match with Laertes, and in its accumulation of tragical results. Well might Fortinbras, coming in peaceful march from recent victory, exclaim —

> "O, proud Death!
> What feast is toward in thine eternal cell,
> That thou so many princes, at a shot,
> So bloodily hast struck?"

Dullness no doubt in us, in early readings of the play, but we confess our indebtedness to Mr. Booth, for the true meaning of a line in Hamlet's last speech. After he has wrested the poisoned cup from Horatio's hand, he says —

> "If thou didst ever hold me in thy heart,
> Absent thee from felicity awhile,
> And in this harsh world draw thy breath in pain,
> To tell my story."

Striving against the poison at work in his own frame, he begs Horatio to *live*, and lifts his hand toward that heaven whither he felt his noble friend would go, saying —

> "Absent thee from felicity awhile."

We have taken more copious notes of Booth's Hamlet than of any other character assumed by him. But in reviewing the miscellany, something of Antony's impatience at the prolixity of his messenger from Rome, prompts us to exclaim: "*Grates me:* the sum!" What is the *sum* of Hamlet; what the personal unity of that marvelous and various life? We venture no opinion. But the total impression left by Mr. Booth's personation, at the time of its occurrence, and which still abides, was that of a spiritual melancholy, at once acute and profound. This quality colored his tenderest feeling and his airiest fancy as well as his graver purpose. You felt its presence even when he was off the stage. As the Claude mirror defines, refines, and tones the landscape, so Booth's impersonation lent a saddened and mysterious charm to the vast world of Hamlet's thought and observation.

SHYLOCK.

The Hebrew blood, which, from some remote ancestor, mingled in the current of his life; and was evidently traceable in his features; and haply determined the family name (Booth from Beth, Hebrew for house, or nest for birds), did also undoubtedly influence Mr. Booth's conception of the character of Shylock.

He made it the representative Hebrew: the type of a race, old as the world. He drew the character in lines of simple grandeur, and filled it with fiery energy. In his hands, it was marked by pride of intellect; by intense pride of race; by a reserved force, as if there centered in him the might of a people whom neither time, nor scorn, nor political oppression could subdue; and which has at successive periods, even down to our own day, drawn the attention of mankind towards its frequent examples of intellectual power. His pronunciation of the words —

> "This Jacob from our holy Abraham was,"

carried the mind back into the remotest antiquity, and begat an involuntary respect for the speaker.

The intense realism of Edmund Kean made Shylock merely a malignant usurer; and so represented, to our thinking, rather Gratiano's idea of the Jew, than Shakespeare's. But Kean, after making the audiance hate him, did, by one of his sudden turns of power, and by the pathos of his voice, in the passage beginning—

> "Nay, take my life and all,"

produce an entire revulsion of feeling in the listener, so that pity took the place of execration.

Booth, on the contrary, whether for better or worse, made usury the Jew's accidental or enforced employment; and avarice, which is the natural ally of such employment, rather a graft on his nature than a part of the original stock. He disdained all appeal to the compassion of his judges. He gave the passage quoted only as a softened expression of that inexorable logic, which in other scenes, yields a certain dignity to the character, and wins our reluctant regard.

Geo. Frederick Cooke, in the passage beginning "Hath not a Jew eyes?" when he came to the word "affections," so informed it with human feeling, so contrasted it with the context, that it remains as the marked point of his performance. But if Kean's abject appeal for the means of living, when Shylock was utterly ruined, be doubtful; Cooke's turning the Jew out of the current of his reasoning wrath, when he had wealth and power, and was rejoicing in the prospect of revenge, — in order to complain of his wounded affections, — seems at best but a tempting error of conception. Booth, on the contrary, gave no prominence to his affections; but did, as we believe Shakespeare intended, evenly include them in that inventory of the qualities and conditions of man, on which Shylock based his claim to be respected as a man.

Shylock develops the strongest traits of his character in the very first scene. Observe the cautious self-satisfaction with which he holds and plies the reins of monetary power, in his interview with Bassanio and Antonio. Yet the Hebrew stands back of and above the usurer. He says, musing on Antonio —

"If I can catch him once upon the hip,
I will feed fat the ancient grudge I bear him.
He hates our sacred nation."

Again —

"What! are there masques? Hear you me, Jessica:
Lock up my doors . . . .
. . . .
Let not the sound of shallow foppery, enter
My sober house."

Perhaps the grandest performance of Shylock ever given by Mr. Booth, or any other, was on the third of September, 1850, during his last engagement before going to California. He was in perfect physical condition. His voice was still capable of that unfathomed resonance, which told in the settled revengeful purpose of the part. The general conception was as we have indicated.

The Third Act opened. Salanio and Salarino are conversing of Antonio's losses. Shylock enters, having just found out Jessica's theft, and heard of her elopement. He should say, "You knew, none so well as you, of my daughter's flight." But no word could we distinguish. His voice seemed molten by passion, before it could be shaped into words, and so leaped from his lips, a volcanic eruption of inarticulate speech.

This as he was coming in. When fairly on the scene, the fire retreats inward. He immediately proves himself an overmatch for the lighter wit of the two Venetian gallants. One of them makes a feeble rally, then they stand silent, and receive without further parley his tremendous questioning.

The fiery scorn he threw into the words

. . . "A bankrupt — a prodigal . . . that *used* to come so smug upon the mart. . . . He was wont to call me *usurer*. Let him look to his bond."

And he strode down the stage to the farthest corner, the white fire of his anger writhing in his face, animating his tread, and flying out in his wild but determinate gesture.

Salarino. "Why I am sure if he forfeit, thou wilt not take his flesh: what's that good for?"
Shylock (*turning suddenly*). "To bait fish withal."

We have heard Mr. Booth, in one of his tamer moods, say this with a gesture as if holding a fishing-rod. But on this occasion, with a gesture inexpressibly violent and rapid, he seemed to be tearing the flesh, and throwing it into the sea.

The whole of the next speech rode on a mighty tide of passion, gathering, accelerating, rushing due on, but broken sometimes by fearful pauses of thought, followed by smiting blows of logic, like the hush before the thunder-stroke. How those questions came, winged and edged with scorn, solid as the substance of thought, fiery and irresistible as the motion of passion!

Nor can we tell from what depth of vigor arose the grand and various expression of the next scene, directly after, on the entrance of Tubal. Let the reader review the text.

> "No ill luck stirring but what lights o' my shoulders. . . . . No tears but o' my shedding."
> "I thank God, I thank God."
> "Good news. Ha! ha! ha!"
> "Thou stickest a dagger in me!"
> "I am glad of it. I'll torture him. I am glad of it."
> "I would not have given it for a wilderness of monkeys."
> "I will have the heart of him if he forfeit."
> "Go, Tubal, and meet me at our *Synagogue*, at our Synagogue, Tubal."

All given with glowing passion, and fine artistic changes.

In the fourth act, Booth enters the court-room, calm, his tumult of passion condensed into a settled purpose; and with a kind of dignity, if unrelenting hate like his can bear that quality. *From* the audience, he listens to the Duke, then quietly begins: —

"I have possessed your Grace of what I purpose;
And by *our holy Sabbath* have I *sworn*
To have the due and forfeit of my bond:
If you deny it, let the danger light
Upon your charter, and your city's freedom."

The last two lines were given with an outreaching and arching motion of the arm and hand, palm downward, like the stoop of a bird of prey.

We feel the pressure of the intense passionate purpose, below the logic, in his short colloquies with Bassanio and Gratanio, and in his longer speeches to the court — till Portia, as the Doctor, enters, and speaks of mercy *and* the law. Against her plea for mercy, as against the twice-blessed quality itself, Shylock sets his face like a flint; but as his religion moved him, at the mention of the name of God, Booth folded his arms upon his breast, and bowed his head in reverence.

"My deeds upon my head!"

exclaims Shylock. As Christ was mercy, there may have been floating in Shakespeare's mind that other fearful imprecation, "His blood be on us and on our children." The dark effluence of the same spirit appears in the language of the Jew. Booth gave the words with solid force, as after, in saying: —

"An oath, an oath, I have an oath in heaven:
Shall I lay perjury upon my soul?
No, not for Venice,"

he stood a type of the religion of the law.

The crisis of the play arrives. Shylock finds his "justice" a two-edged sword, and is suffering from the unexpected stroke of it. Foiled of the penalty he craves, he says: —

"I take this offer then: pay the bond thrice,
And *let* — the *Christian* — *go*," —

uttered between set teeth, and with repeated gesture of repulsion: still holding to the last, his pride of faith as the dominant element of his cruel mind.

IAGO.

An actor is the only innocent hypocrite. That a man of Mr. Booth's probity and generosity of soul, should have so insphered the character of Iago as to make it one of his most admirable and popular representations, is a case in point. Iago seems not so much a debauched intelligence as an intelligence which had been the devil's own from the beginning. Yet his diabolism was not of that kind which delights primarily in others' pain. It consisted rather in an unresting intellectual activity, without moral principle or human feeling.

He is a constitutional liar. He brags of it. In audacious contrast to Him who said, "I am that I am," Iago says, "I am *not* what I am." Danger and crime are necessary to give scope to the action of his fertile brain. He is the embodiment of spiritual wickedness in human character. And we must resort to this paradox, in order to *make* him human; that he seeks for motives, which are in themselves criminal, in order to justify the proceeding of his spontaneous malignity. He is the parent of many a villain in more recent literary art. The Mephistopheles of Goethe is of his family, at the least a cousin-german. But Goethe slights his fiend into heaven, and gives him preternatural power to work mischief on the earth: while Iago's successes (which are only postponed failures) are the mere product of his busy brain, and his plumed-up will. He "works by wit, and not by witchcraft."

Hazlitt says that Kean made Iago "a gay light-hearted monster; a careless, cordial, comfortable villain." Booth gave quite another version. His conception was saturnine; but the expression of it was strangely swift and brilliant. He showed the dense force, the stealth, the velvet-footed grace of the panther; the subtlety, the fascination, the rapid stroke of the fanged serpent. There was less variation in his performances, one from the other, of this part, than he exhibited in the portrayal of any other Shakespearean character. Whatever difference did exist, lay in the greater or less intensity of the representation.

On the 15th of September, 1847, as we most vividly remember, he was possessed by his most splendid devil. He came on the stage, clear as spirit, and the voice he used was that most sweet and audible, deep-revolving bass. He "talked far above singing." His delivery of the text was a masterpiece of colloquial style. It had all the abrupt turns, the tones of nature, the unexpectedness, and the occasional persuasive force, which belong to the best conversation.

In the first scene, having quieted Roderigo's complaints, he breaks out with —

> "Call up her father;
> Rouse *him* (*that is, Othello*), make after him, poison his delight,
> Proclaim him in the streets; incense her kinsmen,
> And though he in a fertile climate dwell,
> Plague him with flies: though that his joy be joy,
> Yet throw such changes of vexation on 't,
> As it may lose some color."

Observe the rapid alternation of subject in these lines, and the chasing up of mischievous suggestion they contain.

> *Roderigo.* Here is her father's house: I'll call aloud.
> *Iago.* Do with like timorous accent and dire yell,
> As when (by night and negligence) the fire
> Is spied in populous cities.

There was no heat in this passage. Booth

uttered it with a devilish unconcern, as if pleased with the fancy of terror and dismay, and playing meanwhile with his sword-hilt, or pulling at his gauntlets. He then strikes on the door of Brabantio's house, and speaking through the key-hole, sounds the resonant alarm, "What, ho, Brabantio!" Yet in saying this, we felt that his mind was "playing with some inward bait." The duplicity, the double nature, the devil in him, was subtly manifest.

After Roderigo has made himself known in the darkness, and while Brabantio, from the window, is uttering his peevish personalities, why cannot some actor who represents the "silly gentleman," make him interrupt the old man at intervals, in order to get a hearing, instead of repeating "Sir, sir, sir," all at once, as is invariably done upon the stage? and which indeed is in the text so set down.

While we are in the mood of complaint, let us note the ludicrous error, usually committed by actors, in Iago's next speech:

> "Zounds, sir, you are one of those that will not serve God, if the devil bid you."

In which they bring down the emphasis

plump on "devil," as if the highest motive for serving God, were the devil's bidding! Booth said: "that will not serve *God*, if the devil *bid* you," giving the plain meaning, that the devil's bidding was no argument *against* serving God.

In the first scene, Iago enters, lying to Roderigo. In the second he enters, lying to Othello about Roderigo. In the third, he is a silent attendant during the trial of Othello's marriage. But no one who saw Mr. Booth in any of these scenes, either speaking or silent, could escape the impression of the presence of a malign and potent intellect.

The second act opens in Cyprus. Desdemona is waiting and anxious for the arrival of Othello. She says: —

> "I am not merry; but I do beguile
> The thing I am by seeming otherwise. —
> Come, how would'st thou praise me?"

In Iago's reply, with his invented rhymes, Booth showed that nature in art, which was one felicity of his genius. He was a poet caught in the very act of invention; with just those pauses, abstractions, flashes, and occasional career of speech, when a line or two came out entire — which befit the passage.

The ambition of many actors is to make the sound an echo to the sense. Booth used his grand voice, not as echo, but as interpreter. His imagination was so penetrative, that he did not stop at the imagery, but voiced the thought or emotion imaged. In simple passages, however, where the ring, or hum, or buzz, or plunge, or clang, or suspiration, of the words, is identical with their meaning, as was the case in the early days of human speech, nothing could exceed the sphered beauty of that tongue's utterance. An example occurred in Iago, on the night in question. He exclaims: "The Moor! I know his trumpet." He gave the word, with the very sound of the instrument; and tossed it from his lips with the careless grace of an accomplished musician. The sound startled from his dull mood one critic in the audience, and kept him an alert listener for the remainder of the play. In the self-betraying soliloquy that concludes this scene, occur the lines —

> "Now I do love her too:
> Not out of absolute lust (though peradventure
> I stand accountant for as great a sin ").

The gratuitous fiendishness contained in this

parenthesis, Booth illustrated, by looking up to heaven with defiant forehead and gesture, and with a cold and mocking smile.

Iago has fooled Roderigo to the top of his bent; made Cassio drunk — too drunk, and vulgarly so, most actors make him — a quarrel follows, the town rises, and Othello appears. Iago is called on for explanation, and finds himself in just those circumstances which give a stinging relish to the motion of his mind. How he stood, still, but with a quick spirit in every fibre, between the roused Othello and the drunken Cassio, vigilant, vital, ready for the unknown emergency, and with an invention whose play was "easy as lying!"

He reached the acme of hypocrisy in the passage beginning —

> "Touch me not so near:
> I had rather have this tongue cut from my mouth
> Than it should do offense to Michael Cassio!"

When left alone with Cassio, Iago says: —

> "As I am an honest man I thought you had received some bodily wound."

The simpler meaning is conveyed, by the usual emphasis on "bodily." But this emphasis would oppose bodily to spiritual wounds, and Iago has no faith in the latter. Booth, with fine penetration, said, "I thought you had received some *bodily wound*," emphasizing both words, as if there were no other wounds to suffer from. And we find him directly after blowing "reputation," the loss of which Cassio so deplores, like a bubble, into thin air.

With what amazing fertility of evil resource has Shakespeare invested Iago: and what subtlety of adaptation did Booth exhibit in those soliloquies, wherein he "plumes up his will;" and in the varied play of faculty he brings to bear on the other characters of the drama! We dare not attempt to analyze his look, tone, manner, the undefinable efflux of wickedness, under the guise of friendship, by which, in the Third Act, he obtains the mastery over Othello's mind. One or two points may bear specific mention. Finding the suspicion he has awakened in the Moor, applies alone to Cassio, leaving Desdemona yet clear of it, Iago says:

> "Good name in man — and woman — dear my lord
> Is the immediate jewel of their souls."

Isolating the words "and woman" by a pause before and after, and completing the isolation by uttering them in an altered, clear, low tone, he aims directly at Othello's heart, and plants in it the first surmise of his wife's infidelity.

His addresses to Othello had a fearful symmetry of falsehood. He lied so like truth, that had we been in Othello's place, we felt he would have deceived us too. His soliloquies, and those looks and slight gestures aside, alone revealed his true character. Between his assumed friendship, and these tokens of self-betrayal, he passed with incredible rapidity of transition; and did it with a keen relish, an intense gust of iniquity. Yet was the odiousness of Iago's nature lightened and carried off by the grace and force of Booth's representation. For, disguise it as we may, the love of power is so natural to man, that we take an unmeasured delight in the exhibition of power, whether for good or evil — in a play. The eyeballs of a just-imported leopard, that we saw in our youth, dilating and glancing with a green malignant light, shine still with all the old fascination; and glow in memory by some occult association, as we write of Booth's Iago. He chastened Shakespeare by delivering, as in one continuous line,

> "It is a common thing to have a foolish wife."

He gave

> "Dangerous conceits . .
> Burn like the mines of sulphur,"

with a voice like a writhing inward flame.

Wherever Shakespeare raised one of his characters above its habitual level, by pluming it with the splendor of his own imagination, Booth instinctively took wing with him; and the manner in which he gave

> "Not poppy nor mandragora
> Nor all the drowsy syrups of the world
> Shall ever medicine thee to that sweet sleep
> Which thou ow'dst yesterday,"

was, as if a boding angel, in tones of profoundest music, banished all the agents of repose, and created the doom he pronounced.

In the night scene, where Roderigo encounters Cassio, on the very night when the deeper tragedy of the play is consummated, Iago appears with a light and a drawn sword. The light shone on Booth's pale and fiendish face, as, with a sword-stroke into Roderigo's wounded body, he delivers himself of this stroke of devilish wit: —

> "Kill men i' the dark!"

It will be remembered that he had instigated Roderigo to the murder of Cassio.

In the last scene, as Iago stands a defeated culprit, his hideous crimes exposed, Othello saying, —

> "If that thou be'st a devil I cannot kill thee,"

runs at and stabs him. Booth replied, staunching the wound, and mastering the anguish of it, and with a look of steady hatred and defiance,

> "I bleed, sir, but — *not* — *killed.*"

As if he would say, "You are right, you cannot kill me. I *am* a devil."

OTHELLO.

DURING a certain week in the autumn of 1847, there came to us a special revelation of the scope of the histrionic art. On Tuesday, September 14th, Mr. Booth enacted Othello. On Wednesday, 15th, Iago — that Iago we have just briefly noticed — and on Thursday, 16th, Othello again. The entireness of transition in so short a span; the completeness of identification in characters so essentially diverse, filled us with a wonder that still abides. But a great actor is the only human being who is voluntarily and happily beside himself, with power of complete self-recovery, and readiness for a fresh transformation.

Booth's Iago was so well known to us; his figure rose so surely in our imagination as we read the play, that we heard, not without some misgiving, the announcement of Mr. Booth as Othello, "the first time for many years." We confess to a fear, lest, in his performance, some look, or trait, or tone of the deep-revolving subtle villainy of his more familiar part might appear, to despoil the frank and noble presence of the Moor. But it is scarcely too much to say, that the two characters did not lie more clearly asunder in the mind of Shakespeare, than in Mr. Booth's representation.

Othello was a Christian graft upon a wild Arabian stock. He was a Mauritanian prince. The Eastern origin of his race; his birth in Africa; his military life; his Venetian culture; all had part in building up a character, compact of strength, fervency, simplicity, and honor. Accordingly, Booth's personation was marked, especially in the earlier portion of the play, by an oriental largeness and calm. Even when his frame of nature is wrenched from its fixed place, by Iago's preternatural enginery, there is a continual recoil and reinstatement of the Moor's solid virtue; so that he never loses our respect, at the same time that he moves our sympathies beyond any other male character in Shakespeare. We might sum up Mr. Booth's characterization in one word — magnanimity.

In this mood of mind he enters on the scene, Iago following. If the reader could imagine Booth's Iago played against his own Othello, how would the illusion we hope to create in him be heightened! Iago tries to incense Othello against Roderigo, the Moor's *soi-disant* rival. Othello answers —

> " 'Tis better — as — it is."

Booth gave this with a gravity, a weighty distinctness on the last three words, which conveyed a reproof, and was intended to dismiss the subject. Iago returns to the charge:

> " Nay, but he prated,
> And spoke such scurvy and provoking terms
> Against your *honor*;" —

a home thrust, but finding it without effect, his speech veers upon Brabantio, his place and power for injury. Then comes from Othello the noble reply, beginning —

> " Let him do his spite.
> . . . .
> I fetch my life and being
> From men of royal siege; and my demerits
> May speak unbonneted to *as* proud a fortune
> As *this* that I have *reached*,"

given with peculiar intonation, and rising emphasis, imparting a fine accent to the meaning, that it did not add to the dignity of a Moorish prince to become the son-in-law of a Venetian senator.

> "For know, Iago,
> But that I love the gentle Desdemona,"

with wealth of tenderness, and sad, as all high feeling is, and in tones that seemed the vibration of his "dear heart-strings." In that speech Mr. Booth struck the key note of the character.

How picturesque and effective are the night scenes of this great play! The whole of the First Act, with its large variety of place and persons, and the whole of the Fifth, with much of the Second and Fourth Acts, pass in the night. Night is the season for peace and love. It is the house of grief. It is the cloak of crime.

Brabantio (entering with followers, torches, and weapons) exclaims—

> "Down with him, thief!"

(They draw on both sides.) Iago strikes in with—

> "You, Roderigo, come sir, I am for you."

Perhaps he intended to pick off that gentleman, whose purse he had already drained, even as he does later in the play. Perhaps in encountering him he only meant to preserve him, in order to pluck him cleaner.

We speculate on the motives and conduct of Shakespeare's characters, as if they were living persons. And with reason; for they are not only living, but immortal. Iago plainly expects a fight. He has no sympathy with that romance of honor, which governs Othello's conduct. He can have no knowledge of it. But so disengaged from all purpose or permission of quarrel is the Moor, that he playfully and nobly says —

"Keep up your bright swords, for the dew will rust them."

Then turning to Desdemona's father, who has just called him "thief," he adds, in a manner of mingled reproof and deference —

"Good signior, *you* shall more command with *years* —
Than with your weapon."

But into the utterance of the last line, there crept a keen, low-toned, cool disdain. The old father insists on Othello's arrest, and heaps gross accusations on him. Then came from Booth —

"The flash and outbreak of a fiery mind,"

in the words —

"Hold your hands!
Both you of my inclining *and* the rest;
Were it my cue to fight, I should have known it
Without a prompter" —

the concluding words quietly addressed to the disappointed Iago.

Charles Lamb said that he was quite unable to measure the value of Hamlet's soliloquy, "To be or not to be," because he had heard it so often recited. Othello's address to the Senate is almost equally hackneyed. But Mr. Booth so cleansed it from the scurf of custom; gave it with such dignity, directness, delicacy, fervor, that we seemed to hear it then for the first time. To genius all doors fly open. He took us into old Brabantio's house, and made us see the very progress of his courtship; and the gentle lady, the house affairs dispatched, sitting a charmed listener to his recital.

> "Her father loved me (*gesture of dissent from the father*);
> Oft invited me:
> Still questioned me the story of my life,
> From year to year, the battles, sieges, fortunes,
> That I have passed.
> I ran it through, even from my boyish days,
> To the very moment that he bade me tell it."

These circumstances were *proof* of love, in the estimate of the frank-minded Moor. In the dramatic truth of Booth's delivery we felt the presence of the "insolent foe," by whom he was "sold to slavery," and the joy of his "redemption thence." Desdemona listens with "greedy ear" —

> "Which I observing,
> Took *once* a pliant hour, and found *good* means"

glancing at the father —

> "To draw from her a prayer of earnest heart,
> That I would all my pilgrimage dilate,
> Whereof by parcels she had something heard,
> But not intentively."

In these words and in the following lines, where he quotes Desdemona, we seem to hear her speaking through him, with all her innocent finesse, and full-hearted tenderness. "'Twas pitiful," as if concluding: then with fresh access of feeling, and with rising inflection, "'*Twas — wondrous — pitiful.*" The address was made to the Senate, and not to the audience. We can only add, in the language of the Duke —

> "I think this tale would win my daughter too."

The reader has undoubtedly remarked, that in making the comparison of excellence in actors, we excluded all literatures beside the English, and all nations who did not speak the English tongue. And simply because of the unquestioned supremacy of Shakespeare. The French and Italian translations, and the actors who perform in them, may be passed by without comment. The Germans, by affinity of language and race, may put in a better claim. The name of Devrient, has a vague high fame, in the German Shakespeare, as well as in the drama of his native land. Travelled scholars have also, for many years, brought back report of the unmatched excellence of Mr. Bogumil Dawison, as a representative of Shakespearean character; and the cultivated audiences of New York and Boston have recently enjoyed the rare pleasure of seeing him play Othello in German, to Mr. Edwin Booth's Iago in English.

We watched his performance with eager interest. It was full of beauties, and strikingly original and natural, in action and by-play. He dismissed Cassio as if he loved him. He lay on a couch in his own chamber, as if no one were looking at him. He hung over his dead wife, in the last scene, uttering cries whose simple pathos touched the heart. His voice is sweet and flute-like, but of little compass, or variety of tone. His facial expression was intense and vivid, though with sameness; and his gestures were indeterminate and heaving. Yet he made one exit, in the great Third Act, in which, by abrupt pauses, and repeated looking back, and by glances, and play of feature, he expressed the contending emotions of Othello's mind, in a manner that Roscius might have envied, and which aimed well at the height of Shakespeare. He introduced the long first scene of the Fourth Act, always omitted on the English and American stage; but which is so necessary to that continuity and accumulation of evidence, which overbears Othello's mind, and hurries on the catastrophe — and for this we thank him heartily. He carried naturalness to an excess. His affection for Desdemona was very manifest — perhaps a little fulsome. It lacked dignity, and that reticence which belongs to calm, firm natures, whose flame of love is contained, intense, and steady. He translated the character, as well as the language, into German.

These remarks will apply to his expression, in that scene we have reached, in our present consideration of the play — the scene of Othello and Desdemona meeting at Cyprus. The words "content," "calm," "comfort," and "content" again, appear in the Moor's first speeches. He calls her his "*soul's* joy." So chaste, so deep-hearted is his love, that he feels a willingness to die, — an experience only possible to the most serene and imaginative mood. We return to Mr. Booth.

> " If it were now to die
> 'Twere now to be most happy; for I fear
> My soul hath her content so absolute,
> That not another comfort like to this,
> Succeeds in unknown fate."

The calm intensity, the purified and exalted passion, the sad, prophetic, far-off music he infused into this passage, can never be forgotten. We shall recall it, once, in the course of this analysis.

On that scene of confusion so skillfully engineered by Iago, — with Cassio drunk, Montano wounded, and the town alarmed, — Othello appears, roused with indignation. The tropic blood, till now sleeping in his veins, begins to stir. He dismissed Cassio, *not* as if he loved him ; or rather as if, loving him, he loved discipline and honor more.

We have had the initial touches of this man's vast capacity for imaginative emotion. We are prepared for the grand Third Act, exhibiting the second distinct phase of Othello's nature, yet without losing his noble individuality. We have hitherto seen him as the Christian soldier. He now appears as the barbaric prince. Africa supplants Venice. The mighty passions, nourished by the sun, where he was born, and which lay slumbering within, imparting, so long as they were kept subdued, a lion-like strength to his character, are here set loose, and lashed into a fearful storm, by the devil-agency of Iago.

In order to save a repetition of names, we shall speak, for the time, of Othello and Booth as one person. They were one, to our apprehension. We note the noble confidence of Othello towards Cassio, whom he sees parting from his wife. "I do believe 'twas he." So opposite was Othello by nature, to the selfish and self-generated passion of jealousy, that it required the repeated subtle probe of Iago's wit before even Cassio could be brought under suspicion.

Othello. "O yes, and went between us very oft," —

given with a hearty and happy remembrance of Cassio's friendship. And not till Iago has, by covert and halting insinuations, brought Othello, who lived by truth, to the agonized question, "What dost thou mean?"

does he dare to implicate Desdemona. He does it then only by suggestion, and in the general words "and woman," pushing that card like an ingenious juggler. Othello takes it, and finds it inscribed with characters of dismay. The fiend follows up his advantage, and wrings from the heart of his victim, in the words "O, misery!" tones that for expression of inward desolation we have never heard equaled.

Yet in the next long speech, we find his shaken manhood partially recovering its poise: —

> "Thinkest thou I'd make a *life* of jealousy?"

The blended modesty and self-respect of manner, in the phrase —

> "Nor from mine own weak merits will I draw
> The smallest fear or doubt of her revolt:
> For she had eyes — and *chose* me."

The word "revolt" was one of those strokes of genius in tone, of which he furnished such numberless examples. It came with access of emphasis, as if he felt, for an instant, how dreadful a thing her revolt might be, then dismisses the thought at once. It was that subtle touch of Iago's, in the phrase —

> "She did deceive her father marrying you,"

put forth as a basis for those "proofs" Othello calls for, which took the ground from under him.

> *Iago.* "I see, this hath a little dashed your spirits."
> *Othello.* "Not a jot. Not a jot,"

in a tone, playing on the surface of a mind, filled with suppressed agony. And again, soon after: —

> "No, not *much* — *moved*,"

till his o'erfraught heart burst into the words:

> "I do not think but Desdemona's honest!"

"Fear not my government," meaning, of course, my self-control, and given with a gesture strangely original and fine — the forefinger of the lifted hand pointed vertically to the top of the head.

> "If I do prove her haggard, etc.,"

in a voice that matched the airy sweep of the imagery; the words, "to prey at fortune," accompanied by a darting and dispersed gesture.

> "Desdemona comes:
> If she be false, O, then heaven mocks itself!
> I'll not believe it."

The sight of his wife dispels suspicion, as daybreak a hideous dream. But the weariness remains.

> "Your napkin is too little."

The handkerchief drops. He goes with Desdemona to the dinner, to which he has invited the "generous islanders." The scene is occupied by Emilia in finding the fatal napkin, and Iago, in snatching it, and plotting mischief with it.

Othello has said —

> "'Tis not to make me jealous,
> To say my wife is fair, feeds well, loves company,
> Is free of speech; sings, plays, and dances well;
> Where virtue is these are more virtuous."

But already, to Othello's mind, Iago has begun to turn that virtue into pitch. And we may imagine the guileless hospitality of the gentle lady to her guests, maddening her husband, so that he abruptly leaves them, and reënters on the scene to Iago, with the exclamation —

> "Ha, ha! false to me? to *me?*"

He seeks a wretched refuge in the surmise of ignorance: —

> "I had been — happy, if the general camp,
> Pioneers and all" —

the voice of desperation as he heaps up the hyperbole!

> "Had tasted her sweet body,
> So I had nothing known."

But the self-wounding, scorpion mood is of brief duration. With entire change of manner, in a style large, oriental, he came down the stage; and looking towards the listeners, but never at them, he poured the full volume of his voice, not loud but deep, into the "farewell." The melancholy grandeur of the lines, however uttered, finds its way into every soul. In the mere word "farewell," his great heart seemed to burst as in one vast continuing sigh. The phrase, "the tranquil mind," immediately succeeding, came in clear brain-tones, with a certain involved suggestiveness of meaning almost impossible to define, but as if the tranquil mind *had* flown. The whole passage, with its successive images of glorious war, filing and disappearing before his mind's eye, employed some of the grandest elements of voice, subdued to retrospective and mournful cadences.

"Othello's occupation's gone."

And he stood with a look in his large blue eyes — the bronzed face lending them a strange sadness — as if all happiness had gone after. Kean's manner, in this scene, was very different. At the close of the "farewell," he raised both hands, clasped them, and so brought them down upon his head, with a most effective gesture of despair. But the action seems to us like transforming Othello into Edmund Kean.

It is the setting of the "farewell," the grand pause in the passion of the play — like the ominous pause of the maelstrom, at the turning of the tide — which gives it such sway over the mind. The passion returns with redoubled power, to the evident surprise, and almost to the discomfiture of Iago, whom Othello seizes by the throat, demanding ocular proof of his wife's infidelity. The villain can make only short protests. Words can but faintly indicate the terrific and cumulative energy of the passage, beginning —

> "If thou dost slander her, and torture me,
> Never pray more;"

marked as it was equally by intellectual clearness, heat of passion, and imaginative realization. The fit passes, and leaves him in a whirl of doubt; but of doubt pressing towards resolution, demanding proof, and Iago is ready with his master stroke, the —

> "Strong circumstance
> Which leads directly to the door of truth" —

the handkerchief.

> "Such a handkerchief
> (I am sure it was your wife's) did I to-day
> See Cassio wipe his beard with."

When Mr. Booth played Iago, he did, in saying this, while pretending to lay his hand on his heart, to enforce asseveration, tuck away more securely in his doubtlet, the very handkerchief, which, with fiendish purpose, he intended Cassio *should* wipe his beard with.

Now appears the third distinct phase of Othello's nature, the oriental. The history of that handkerchief arises in the mind of the Moor, and with it the dim and dominating superstitions of the East, the birthplace of his race. He exclaims —

> "Now do I *see* 'tis true!"

The passion of the Third Act is so intense and varying, the drain on the physical power of the actor, especially his voice, is so enormous that eight lines, beginning —

> "Like to the Pontic sea,"

have been cut out of the representation. Edmund Kean never gave them. Mr. Booth omitted them on his first performance; but at the urgent solicitation of personal friends, restored them on the second. Their utterance overpaid expectation. They came with headlong speed and vast momentum. The images and names of those eastern seas, he endowed with a peculiar freshness and surprise. "Hellespont" sounded like a torrent dashed on rocks.

> "Till that a capable and wide revenge
> Swallow them up,"

gave the sound, and figured the very action of engulfing waves.

The waters of the river Rhone, as they leave the lake of Geneva, are singularly pure. The turbid Arve empties into the Rhone; and, side by side, without mingling, flow the two distinct currents in the same channel. Even so was it with Othello's mind. The current of his pure and inextinguishable love, runs side by side, without mingling, with the flow of foul and bloody thoughts poured into his heart by Iago. He blows his love to heaven in one pathetic breath. He invokes his love to yield up its crown and hearted throne to tyrannous hate. His bosom swells with its fraught of "aspic's tongues." He passes from the scene, in order to provide —

> "Some swift means of death,
> For the fair devil."

But when he comes, in the very next scene, into the angel presence of his wife, all is changed. He takes Desdemona's hand with a grave tenderness. His paternal, monitory tones, ring clear and sad in our memory.

> "This hand is moist, my lady."
> *Desdemona.* "It yet has felt no age, nor known no sorrow."
> *Othello.* "This argues fruitfulness, and liberal heart:
> Hot, hot, and moist. This hand of yours requires
> A sequester from liberty, fasting and prayer."

This line and the following, remind one of the Hebrew poetry, which consisted of a varied repetition of the thought, in mated lines, but without rhyme. He goes on —

> "Much castigation, exercise devout;"

and he held up the innocent hand between his two, in momentary but fervent attitude of prayer. Then, still holding her hand in one of his, and pointing with the other, and looking keenly but without unkindness into her palm, he adds, with heightening and ringing accent: —

> "For here 's a young and sweating devil here,
> That commonly rebels."

These three words in changed tone, and with the voice sustained at the close, and given in such a manner that the attentive listener supplemented the meaning — "and I fear must do so in your case." So, at the first performance. On the second, a fine variation —

> "For here 's a young and sweating —*devil* here,"

with the same searching intensity; then a kindly doubt seems to rise in his mind, and he gives her the benefit of it in saying —

> "That *commonly* (slight pause) *rebels.*"

The history of the handkerchief, containing the only touch of the supernatural in this domestic tragedy, was told with a fine oriental fanaticism.

> "She was a charmer, and could almost read
> The thoughts of people."

Eye, gesture, voice, conspired to give the very impress of divination.

> "And bid me, when my fate would have me wive."

His look reached upward, as a Chaldean's might, towards those stars which influence human destiny.

> "Make it a darling, like your precious eye."

The priceless, unreplaceable preciousness of the handkerchief, was condensed in the word "darling," with a keen, fond, defended intonation.

> *Desdemona.* "Is it possible?"
> *Othello (instantly).* "'Tis *true.* There's magic in the web of it.
> A sibyl, that had numbered in the world
> The sun to make two hundred compasses,
> In her *prophetic fury* — sewed the work."

The whole passage came with a frenzy of spontaneous narration; and with gesture full of subtle intimations, not mimicries, — for example, turning, swift as a swallow in flight, from the inspiration of the sibyl, to the sewing of the work.

> "Fetch it; let me see it,"

as with a desperate certainty that it could not be found or brought.

It argued a certain badness of nature in Emilia, for which only her wakened conscience and her willing death at the end of the play might fully atone, that she could bear to stand by and hear this relation, witness her mistress's astonished grief, and Othello's angry exit, and yet withhold the little word that would have set all right.

The omission of the first scene of the Fourth Act, was a serious fault. It should always be presented. In it the simulated proofs thicken. The wild alternation of love with jealous madness in Othello — that parenthesis of contemplation, where he refers his "shadowing passion" to "instructed nature," and not to Iago's report; and so makes the very emotion he suffers under an occult proof of his wife's guilt — the bloody thoughts which clot into single, terrible words — his trance — are all of the closest texture of dramatic situation and expression, and can employ the very highest genius of any actor. Moreover, that scene prepares the auditor for the following, and accounts for Othello's direct and cruel accusations. The turbid current has mingled with the pure.

We come now to the last scene — the bed-chamber. It was full of fate. Mr. Booth entered with an eastern lamp lighted in one hand, and a drawn scimitar in the other. The oriental subjective mood had obtained full possession of him. The supposed "proofs" had sunk into his mind, and resolved themselves into a fearful unity of thought and purpose. This is fully shown in a later speech:

"For to deny each article — *with oath*,
Cannot remove or choke the strong conception
That I do groan withal. Thou art to die."

And again: "Being done (i. e., *resolved on*) there is no pause" (*in deed*).

The expression of contained energy in his movement, the large, low-toned, vibrant rumination of his voice, sounding like thought overheard, filled the scene with an atmosphere at once oppressive and fascinating.

> "I know not where is that *Promethean* heat,"

as if the adjective had just occurred to him; and accompanied by a wandering and questioning gesture.

We feel a certain shame in picking out items for comment from scenes of profound or exalted passion, like this one we have in view; and especially as the excellence of Mr. Booth's acting could not be measured by the number of good points he made, but by the entireness of identification. Yet we find no help for it. Observe the eastern imagery employed throughout this scene. The "chaste stars;" the "error of the moon;" "the Arabian trees;" "the base Indian;" the "huge eclipse of sun and moon;" and that big imagination of the world as —

> "One entire and perfect chrysolite."

The deed is done. Emilia enters:

> "O good my lord, yonder 's foul murder done."
> *Othello.* "What, now?"
> *Emilia.* "But now, my lord."
> *Othello.* "It is the very error of the moon;
> She comes *more near* the earth than she was wont,
> And makes men mad."

His gesture seemed to figure the faith of the Chaldean, and to bring the moon more near. "Roderigo killed!" (*with wonder*). "And Cassio killed!" (*glutting the words in his throat*).

> "O, I were damned beneath all depth in hell,
> But that I did proceed, upon just grounds,
> To this extremity."

He uttered that first tremendous line with burning intensity. Milton has borrowed the thought, and put it into the mouth of Satan:

> "And in the lowest depth, a lower deep," etc.

After the truth is out, and under the spell of his grand presence, and in the tragic continuity of the scene, his speech over his dead wife seemed the ultimate reach of blended grief and love and wild remorseful passion of which the human voice is capable.

> "Wash me in steep-down gulfs of liquid fire!"

Othello has wounded Iago, but not killed him. He says: —

> "I am not sorry neither: I'd have *thee*—*live;*
> For in my sense, 'tis happiness to die."

We now recall that passage in the Second Act—

> "If it were now to die
> 'Twere now to be most happy."

Then, the expression came from the absolute fullness of his joy; now, the same word tells of the last bitterness of his grief and self-condemnation:

> "The wheel has come full circle."

From this moment his own death is assured.

At the summons, "Bring him away," and as he is beginning his final speech—

> "Soft you; a word or two before you go,"

he takes a silken robe, and carelessly throws it over his shoulder; then reaches for his turban, possessing himself of a dagger he had concealed therein.

> "Then must you speak
> Of one that loved, not wisely, but too well,
> . . . .
> . . . . . Of one whose hand,
> Like the base Indian, threw a pearl away
> Richer than all his tribe."

He uttered the word "pearl" as if it were indeed "the immediate jewel of his soul," his wife, with a lingering fullness and tenderness of emphasis, and with a gesture as if, in the act of throwing it away, he cast his own life from him.

If the excellence of a performance may be judged by its effect on the audience, this one had transcendant merit. Let the hushed attention of a company unusually numerous and refined — let the silent tears of strong men, carried by the imaginative stress of the scene beyond the reaches of their critical culture — bear witness. For ourself, we went no more to the play during that engagement; but walked about as in a voluntary dream, not caring to dispel by attendance on even *his* other performances, the pathetic illusion he had created.

MACBETH.

Among those undefined influences which stream from the greater dramas of Shakespeare may be numbered the climate of the play; and this, while often eluding the observation, tells surely upon the feeling of the reader. From tropical heat, we pass to the chill mists of Scotland. From the alternate languor and fierceness of passion — from imagination which rides upon the current of the blood, and revels in gorgeous color and in rich and sensuous forms, we pass to that higher imagination, which allies itself to the intellectual and spiritual nature; in a word, from the atmosphere of Othello to the atmosphere of Macbeth.

The ductile flame of Mr. Booth's histrionic genius passed into this northern form with even greater readiness and radiance than into Othello. The supernatural element in Macbeth is more pervading and various in its working than in Hamlet. The character is more closely knit; the action more peremptory and progressive. In his ambition, and in the ways of satisfying it, there are points of likeness to Richard. But Richard moved toward his design "without remorse or dread," while Macbeth is a victim to both these conditions; not from a lack of courage, but by virtue of a morbid excess of imagination, which projects his thoughts into objects. So dominant is this quality, that the weird sisters themselves seem like the outward shapes of his guilty purposes. They appear first upon the scene, then vanish, then reappear, as if they were the influences of his mind as well as the heralds of his approach.

Mr. Booth filled this part. We had seen gracious performances, and heard musical readings of the text by other actors. They *reported* the character. Booth was possessed by it. A captain in the service of his king, and returning from successful fight, in company with Banquo, he is met upon a blasted heath by the three witches. The preternatural grandeur, and significant brevity, of their greeting, are usually lost upon the stage. And this, we contend, is owing quite as much to the incapacity of imagination on the part of the performer of Macbeth, as to the fantastical, half-comic aspect of the three old women. While they were speaking, Mr. Booth betrayed his strong inward agitation; and when they vanished (that is, clattered off the stage), he looked at them, then into the air, with a quick and wonder-struck transition, which volatilized their substance, and abolished their defect.

We must illustrate this scene by a comparison.

Banquo. "The earth hath bubbles, as the water has,
And these are of them. Whither are they vanished?"
Macbeth. "Into the air; and what seemed corporal melted
As breath into the wind."

Mr. Vandenhoff, the elder, a gentleman whose readings from Shakespeare and other poets delighted large audiences in this country some twenty years since, had a voice singularly sweet and sonorous. We saw him act Macbeth, or rather heard him read the part; for his action was always secondary. His delivery of the passage quoted, was a marvel of descriptive intonation. He gave body and form to the impalpable air. You could almost see his breath in it. But he did *not* give the vanishing. Booth did. With a sudden upward look, and with a sudden springing tone, not musical, but like the whiz of a shaft from a cross-bow, he gave "*into* the *air*." Could he dally with the image? No. Voice, look, action, conveyed the instant thought, the vanishing. And the conclusion of the sentence came in the same style:

> "And what seemed corporal" (*looking at his own body*),
> "*Melted* as *breath* into the *wind*" (*short i*),

with a succession of emphasis, swift, and filled with wonder. To assign the method of various actors, we might say: Vandenhoff played the imagery; Macready, the analysis; Kean, the passion of the scene; Booth, the character, which not only includes the other methods, but supplies an element wanting in them.

The speech beginning—

> "Two truths are told,"

drew upon that well-spring of imaginative expression, which lay deep in Booth's nature, and which Macbeth gave scope for, in a more condensed and terrific way, than any other character. The effect of the "supernatural soliciting" was to kindle this quality into its highest life. No voice that we have ever heard or read of, could convey like his, the unbodied beauty or terror of supernatural emotions. The music of the "imperial theme" was in his ears. He saw the throne in vision, but between him and it were darkness, fearful guilt, and "horrible imaginings."

"My thought, *whose* murder — yet — is but fantastical (*with tone and gesture, that figured a hovering and vanishing shape*),
Shakes so my single state of man (*with vibrant intensity*), that function
Is smothered in surmise, and nothing is
But what is not."

This phrase was uttered in one continuous tone of involved resonance, and in such a manner as to make the listener feel that the thronging shapes of Macbeth's roused and guilty imagination had displaced the world of objective realities.

In that terrific invocation by Lady Macbeth to the —

"Spirits
That tend on mortal thoughts,"

she says,

"Stop up the access and passage to remorse;
That no compunctious visitings of nature
Shake my fell purpose, nor keep peace (?) between
The effect and it."

All the editions, including Hudson's, which for the profound value of its commentary, is, in our judgment, by far the best — preserve this reading. But it would seem that Shakespeare wrote "pace," not "peace." He personifies "nature," whose "visitings" are imagined to "*keep pace*," like a sentinel on guard, between the "effect," the murder, and "it," the fell purpose; sundering them, the very thing Lady Macbeth deprecated.

She welcomes her returning husband with —

> "Great Glamis, worthy Cawdor!
> Greater than both by the all-hail hereafter!"

But his mind is bewildered, and his will weakened, by images of terror his ambition has conjured up. His uncertain and postponing mood, found fit interpretation in the manner of Mr. Booth's delivery of the few words that conclude this scene; and in the soliloquy, beginning —

> "If 'twere done when 'tis done,"

that mood found full utterance. Note the crowd and jostle of inconsequent thoughts, in words that defy punctuation. His mind flies at a tangent, from the need of despatch in the horrid deed he contemplates, to the hope of success; then to fears of the life to come, followed by fears of retribution in the life that now is. Mr. Booth did not play the trumpet stop of his voice, in the phrase —

> "Will plead like angels, trumpet-tongued,"

but gave us rather to feel the gracious nature of Duncan, and —

"The deep damnation of his taking off."

But at length, through the agency of his wife, he is resolved, and strained up to the purpose of regicide. In the dark chamber from which he goes to kill the king, appears before him, the dagger of the mind. The pause, the look, the evasion of the object, which still haunted his vision, and would not pass, as expressed by Booth, bettered nature. At length came the words —

"*Is* this a dagger that I see before me,"

low-toned, scarce audible, with a prolonged emphasis on the first word, and in that manner as if thinking aloud without auditors, which marked all his soliloquies. The whole speech was given in volumed whispers. It was filled with fearful shadows. It made one hold his breath in dreadful expectation, as the actor passed silently —

"With Tarquin's ravishing strides,"

towards the king's chamber.

What an awful grandeur is in this play; with its dense thought, rapid action, substantive imagination, and mystery of iniquity! Even Lady Macbeth, ambitious realist as she was, sometimes thinks in images; as when, in the appalling scene now opening, and which we are disposed to describe by indirection, she speaks of the "surfeited grooms."

> "I have drugged their possets
> That Death and Nature do contend about them,
> Whether they live or die."

In the progress of the scene, her cruel hardness returns, and stands out strong against the overwhelming imaginative remorse of her husband. He not only "peoples the void air with his own phantoms," but fills it with strange voices.

> "Methought I heard a voice cry, 'Sleep no more!
> Macbeth does murder sleep; the innocent sleep,
> . . . .
> Balm of hurt minds.'"

What wealth of meaning in these words! And what assuaging fullness of comfort, Booth infused into that little word, "balm!" "Hurt minds," given in anguished brain-tones.

Goethe pregnantly said, "The power of art lies, not in reporting, but in *conveying* your impressions." We invoke the aid of that power, in our endeavor to convey the actor's manner, in the culminating speech of this scene. Lady Macbeth has gone to gild the faces of the grooms with Duncan's blood. Left alone, Macbeth hears a knocking at the gate.

> "Whence is that knocking?
> How is't with me, when every noise appals me?
> What hands are here? Ha! they pluck out mine eyes!
> Will all great Neptune's ocean wash this blood
> Clean *from* my hand?"

Looking on his hands with starting eyes, and a knotted horror in his features; and wiping one hand with the other *from* him, with intensest loathing. The words came, like the weary dash on reef rocks, and as over sunken wrecks and drowned men, of the despairing sea.

> "No: this my hand will rather
> The multitudinous seas incarnardine,
> Making the green — one red."

He launched the mysterious power of his voice, like the sudden rising of a mighty wind from some unknown source, over those "multitudinous seas," and they swelled and congregated dim and vast before the eye of the mind. Then came the amazing word, "incarnardine," each syllable ringing like the stroke of a sword, and, as it were, "*mak-*

ing the green — one red." The whole passage was of unparalleled grandeur; and in tone, look, action, conveyed the impression of an infinite and unavailing remorse.

During the alarm at the discovery of the murder of the king, Macbeth goes to Duncan's chamber and returns, saying —

> "Had I but died an hour before this chance
> I had lived a blessed time," etc.

While delivering this speech, and the following one, wherein he justifies himself for the added murder of the grooms, an intelligent reporter for the press happened to enter the theatre. "That 's not good!" he exclaimed. "What 's the matter with Booth to-night?" Nothing was the matter, except that the actor had reached the height of the histrionic art, and was speaking Macbeth's *false* sentiments with *pretended* feeling. He delivered the forced imagery, in the affected manner of a hired mourner, hired by "the common enemy of man," and paid — a crown.

Hazlitt says of Kean's Macbeth, that "he was deficient in the poetry of the character;" and that "he did not look like a man who had encountered the Weird Sisters." How then, we may ask, could he play the part at all? For, unless we are made to feel that the actor is possessed by visions of the mind, startled by voices in the air, waylaid, and drawn on to his confusion, by those —

> "Secret, black, and midnight hags,"

it becomes of little account that he gives, as Kean did, one heart-rending picture of remorse, after the commission of a murder. This might be done, without representing Macbeth.

Booth's performance, on the contrary, was constituted by imagination, kindled and swayed by supernatural agencies. Macbeth's action is a succession of crimes, but the intervals are filled with thoughtful speech. The truth and beauty that slide into these musings, show the native affinity of the imaginative faculty with what is best in man. A fine example occurs in these lines: —

> "Duncan is in his grave;
> After life's fitful fever, he sleeps well.
> Treason has done his worst: nor steel, nor poison,
> Malice domestic, foreign levy, nothing,
> Can touch him further."

The mood was profoundly retrospective, but the thoughts it generates were uttered with spontaneous life. The "fitful fever," "treason," "steel," "poison," and the other enemies of life, came as fresh thoughts, not as remembered words. The passage was begun, and closed, and rounded in with tones of mournful music.

In the banquet scene, Banquo personated his own ghost, by appearing in bodily form, and pointing to his wounds. This rank expedient might have been toned into art, by means of costume, obscured lights, and especially by a judicious wonder in the faces and manner of the guests, at the outbreak of Macbeth's supernatural fear of an object *they do not see.* We prefer, however, the visionary Banquo, the pure creation of the usurper's wicked conscience —

> "That coineth goblins swift as frenzy thoughts."

Mr. Booth had to do with the bodily presence, and it must be confessed he spiritualized it strangely. His passion of blended terror and fury, made the object a "horrible shadow," and left it so, as it disappeared.

> "Can such things be
> And overcome us, like a summer's cloud,
> Without our special wonder?"

What is the meaning of these lines? The

cool commentator says nothing, or replies — " Pass over us without wonder, as a casual summer's cloud passes unregarded." But the actor, aglow or chilled with the passion of the scene, gave quite another version. The " summer's cloud " was to him a huge shadow, suddenly scaling the heavens, charged with lightning, and filling the spectator with fear. He used " overcome " in the sense proximate to " overwhelm," or " stoop upon." The speech is made in answer to his wife, who has left the feast and come to his rescue. The vanished ghost still has him in possession, and he turns to his guests, with —

> " You make me strange,
> Even to the disposition that I owe,
> When now I think *you* can behold such sights,
> And keep the natural ruby of your cheeks,
> When mine are blanched with fear,"

and filling the speech with an intense and varied fury of wonder.

The same power of imagination that conjured up the " unreal mockery," played also in the subtile shades of meaning he infused into the passage, beginning —

> " It will have blood."

This was uttered as soliloquy, his wife sitting

silent by. The first phrase came in a resonant murmur, like an assent to a decree of fate. Then, in livelier tone —

> " *They say* — blood will have blood ;
> Stones have been known to move, and trees to speak ; "

given as vivid conceptions, not as recalled impressions. In the concluding phrase of this speech —

> " The secret'st man of blood,"

the word " secret'st " came with so profound and quiet an intonation, that we feared the emphasis it manifestly requires, must be lost. But beneath the lowest depth of his voice, there might at any time open a lower deep ; and here, after a momentary pause, the close listener caught distinctly from some unfathomed source the syllabled rumination—

> " *Man* of blood."

Among those passages of solemn beauty, which find or make their place side by side with the warlike speech of the later scenes, that one following the death of the queen was the most significant. Macbeth is left alone in the world. Life, which had seemed to him before that event of little value, becomes a " walking shadow." The sense of vague desolation which the actor conveyed in this phrase, and in the whole speech to which it belongs, can bear no closer comment:

> "What 's he,
> That was not born of woman? such a one
> Am I to fear, or none."

The word "fear" was uttered in an upward flight of sound, and carried with it a *scorn* of fear. A similar example occurred in Lear:

> "Through tattered clothes small vices do *appear*."

His voice flashed the appearance. Yet no one could on such examples found a rule of elocution. There is no rule for sympathy; none for imaginative art.

> "I bear a charmed life which must not yield
> To one of woman born."

The word "charmed" was not broken in two, as it is usually pronounced, but uttered in one prolonged, resonant, confident syllable.

So close was Mr. Booth's identification of character that its transpirations were manifest, in minor and unconsidered ways. We may instance as contrasted examples the different modes of fighting and dying, in Richard and in Macbeth. The circumstances are externally similar. In each play a brave and guilty king dies in single combat, either with the rightful heir to the throne, or his representative, after suffering a supernatural and prophetic visitation. But how different is the soul of the respective scenes. In Richard, the vision of the night has passed like a forgotten dream. In the battle —

> "A thousand hearts are swelling in his bosom."

His kingdom is still at stake. The hope of victory lives in the fast embrace of his enormous and tenacious will, and never leaves him till the last blow is struck. Accordingly, Booth as Richard, seemed —

> "Treble sinewed, hearted, breathed,
> And fought maliciously,"

while in Macbeth, he flung out voice and action, with the desperate abandonment of a brave soldier, consciously meeting a preternatural doom.

LEAR.

WHAT audacity of genius, or what ignorance of the greatness of the task could have induced Mr. Booth, at the age of twenty-three, to study and represent the character of Lear, we need not now inquire. His success in the personation is a fact of dramatic history. Hazlitt says, under date of April, 1820: "We have seen Mr. Booth's Lear with great pleasure. Mr. Kean's is a greater pleasure to come (so we anticipate)." But the critic has left it on record, that these "expectations were very considerably disappointed;" and he goes on in his brilliant way, through several pages, descanting on the grandeur of the character, and marking in scene after scene, "the deficiency and desultoriness of the interest excited" by Mr. Kean's performance of it. This sounds like implicit testimony from an unwilling witness to the superiority of Booth's Lear. At any rate, it sets the absurd question of imitation — a question first put by prejudice, and since repeated by dullness — entirely at rest; as Booth's performance came *first* in order of time, took place when he was very young, and when Kean was in the full maturity of his powers.

Indeed, as the public mind was preoccupied by Booth's admired personation, there was danger that Kean himself, when he came to play the part, might be regarded as the imitator. And this consideration led him into perverse readings, which are duly scored by Hazlitt's caustic pen. The critic, however, could not dismiss his favorite without giving Booth one disparaging touch, in the following sentence: "In a subsequent part Mr. Kean did not give to the reply of Lear —

'Ay, every inch a king!'

the same vehemence and emphasis that Mr. Booth did, and in this he was justified; for, in the text, it is an exclamation of indignant irony, not of conscious superiority; and he immediately adds with deep disdain, to prove the nothingness of his pretensions —

'When I do stare, see how the subject quakes.'"

From this sentence, judicially pronounced, we appeal to the judgment of the thoughtful reader. Lear has just entered on the scene, fantastically dressed with flowers; and with the exclamation —

> "No, they cannot touch me for coming:
> I am the king himself."

No irony here, but downright mad earnest. Directly after, in reply to Gloster's question —

> 'Is 't not the king?"

the sense of outraged majesty, which, complicated with filial ingratitude, was the very occasion of his madness, comes back on him in a full tide of consciousness, as he exclaims —

> "Ay, every inch a king!"

Hazlitt infers the irony from the line which follows —

> "When I do stare, see how the subject quakes."

To sustain his view there should be some "subject" present who pays the king no respect. There is none. The only other occupants of the scene are Edgar and his blind father, who stand by filled with grief and reverence.

> *Edgar.* "O, thou side-piercing sight!"
> *Gloster.* "O, let me kiss that hand!"

Lear is talking to the shadows of his distempered fancy, which become realities to him. He goes on —

"I pardon that man's life," etc.

In the year 1835, fifteen years after these first performances in London, it was our privilege, in early youth, to see Mr. Booth enact Lear, at the National Theatre in Boston. We saw him then for the first time. The blue eye; the white beard; the nose in profile, keen as the curve of a falchion; the ringing utterance of the names, "Regan," "Goneril;" the close-pent-up passion, striving for expression; the kingly energy; the affecting recognition of Cordelia in the last act — made a deep impression on our boyish mind. We saw and heard all this, but we did not see Lear. We were not old enough.

A closet study of the great poet, coupled with the reading of Charles Lamb's refined and ingenious strictures on the capacity of the stage, conspired to prevent our attendance on a representation of either Hamlet or Lear, during the lapse of many years. The grandeur and subtlety of Mr. Booth's performance in other characters, however, led us one night to dare his Hamlet. We found the atmosphere of the play-house not stifling to the imagination, provided there was genius on the stage. Lamb's fantastic theory vanished. The illumination which accompanied Booth's Hamlet, filled us with eagerness to witness his Lear.

We hold the just representation of this character to be the sublime of the actor's art. "There be players that we have seen play, and heard others praise, and that highly," who, whether developed among us, or arriving from over sea with their budget of literary credentials, did little else in Lear, but show us the choler or the querulousness of an old king, abused and abandoned of his children. They yielded to the temptation of rendering the stormier passages with melodramatic fury, and the milder ones with the peevish feebleness of age. Mr. Kean seems to have overdone the part in both these respects. But overdoing, on the stage, is usually the result of under-thinking. And if there be one character in Shakespeare which requires in an actor fullness of thought, delicacy and subtlety of apprehension, and beyond these, the imaginative and identifying power, it is the character of Lear.

Mr. Macready gave us a scholastic performance, which we witnessed with a certain pleasure. It was marred by the cold premeditation which marked all the efforts of that educated gentleman. It did not move us. Marvelous as was the imitation of the signs of passion, we felt the absence of the pulse of life. He was the intellectual showman of the character, not the character itself. He never got inside. Conception is a blessing not vouchsafed to actors of his school.

With Mr. Booth the case was different. We expected that he would retouch and revivify the dim old pagan figure, and we were not disappointed. He filled the hitherto empty niche. The grandeur of mind, rising colossal and unexpected out of age and destitution; the frenzy of outraged feeling in this child-changed father, passing upward from a poignant sense of his own suffering, and enlarging to a sublime contemplation of the abuses of the world; the gradual untying of that "knot intrinsicate" which bound up his faculties in strength and sanity; the anguish; the pathos; and, through all, the essential kingliness — in a word, the interior life of Lear, came forth and shone in the focal light of Mr. Booth's representation.

In the first scene we note the choleric and impatient majesty of the old king; who yet, out of his deeper love, parleys with Cordelia; hears her cool answers; controls his rising passion, till at length it bursts all bounds, and he casts her off in the speech beginning —

> " Thy truth then be thy dower."

This, and the banishment of Kent, who takes her part, employed the most sonorous elements of Mr. Booth's voice, shaken and weighted as with age, yet betraying latent physical vigor, and choked in passages by the force of contending emotions. We hold the show of vigor to be necessary to the identity of this character, enabling Lear to bear the stress and strain on both body and mind, to which he is afterwards destined; and responding to the wonder expressed in a later scene, when he is turned out in the storm, that his —

> " Life and wits *at once*
> Had not concluded all."

When Goneril, putting aside the mask of filial piety, first assumes the governess, Mr. Booth seemed stunned as with a blow. Then partially recovering, he put those fearful questions — "Are you our daughter?" "Does any here know me?" "Who is it that can tell me who I am?" and the rest in a manner as if freighted with the possibility of madness. The agony of mind, the terrible suspicion just waking in him that he has dispossessed himself irrevocably, the bursts of anger —

> "Degenerate bastard! I'll not trouble thee;"

the selfish regret —

> "Woe that too late repents!"

the affectionate regret —

> "O, most small fault,
> How ugly didst thou in Cordelia show;"

the imperious impatience towards Albany; the desperation, as he strikes his head —

> "O, Lear, Lear, Lear,
> Beat at this gate, that let thy folly in,
> And thy dear judgment out;"

those manifold flaws and starts, all crowded into a few lines, and a few moments, were rendered as they were conceived, with wonderful variety and truth. Even in this whirlwind of his passion, how fine and kingly the courtesy of his reply to Albany, who disclaims all knowledge of what had moved him, in the words —

> "It may be so, my lord."

(So again at the end of the play, in a scene unhappily omitted by Mr. Booth, Lear speaks to Albany —

> "Pray you, undo this button. Thank you, sir;"

the phrase receiving an exquisite accent of courtesy, from the infinite pathos of the situation.)

Then comes the imprecation on Goneril. It is customary to call it "the curse." This word roughens the sense of it unnecessarily. It is in substance a pagan prayer, that she may be childless; but "if she must teem," that her child may be a —

> "Thwart disnatured torment to her;"

that she may suffer the same kind and quality of anguish which she is now inflicting on her father. The principle of the prayer is "an eye for an eye." Putting "Jehovah" instead of "Nature," a Jew might have uttered it. Mr. Booth began it as a solemn adjuration to the unseen power of Nature. The indignant bitterness in the terms of imprecation, seemed as if it was converted out of sweetest images of what a child should be, that lay in the core of his fatherly heart. This double action of his mind, in the agony which it involved, swayed and shook his kneeling figure and lent his voice a wild vibration that drew involuntary sympathy and awe. The heart followed him as he arose and ran out with extended arms. Lear reënters, and in the course of his speech to Goneril, in a similar vein of feeling, but with that change suggested by the lines—

> "That these hot tears which break from me perforce,
> Should make thee worth them —"

Mr. Booth produced one of those large effects which distinguished his personations.

> "Thou shall find
> That I'll resume the shape which thou dost think
> I have cast off forever."

Into the word "resume," he cast the whole energy of his royal will, with a volumed, prolonged, and ringing intonation. His very figure seemed to dilate with majesty.

There is a scene, omitted on the stage, at the end of this First Act, which rivals in pathos that omitted scene in Othello, which we commented on in our notice of that part. It consists of a brief dialogue between Lear and the Fool. The Fool's talk, "matter and impertinency mixed," is partly responded to by Lear, whose few musing "asides," and broken exclamations, touch the core of the plot, and point to the tragic consummation. Let the reader ponder this scene, if he would pass into the presence of the character.

In the opening scene with Regan, in the Second Act, all the unexpressed tenderness which the old king had felt for his best-loved child Cordelia, seemed to pass by a kind of vicarious deflection upon Regan, *now* his only fatherly hope.

> *Regan.* "I am glad to see your highness."
> *Lear.* "Regan, I think you are! I know what reason
> I have to think so; if thou should not be glad,
> I would divorce me from thy mother's tomb,
> Sepulchring an adultress. Beloved Regan,
> Thy sister 's naught. O, Regan, she hath tied
> Sharp-toothed unkindness like a vulture, here; —
> I can scarce speak to thee."

When coldly advised to return to Goneril he says —

> "*Ask — her — forgiveness?*"

Then, with mock humility —

> "Dear daughter, I confess that I am old," etc.

And, when still pressed to return, he rises from his knees with the tremendous exclamation —

> "Never, Regan:
> She hath abated me of half my train;
> Looked black upon me; struck me with her tongue,

> Most serpent-like, upon the very heart:
> All the stored vengeances of heaven fall
> On her ingrateful top."

In these passages, and in the recurrence to his desperate hope in Regan —

> " Thy tender hefted nature shall not give
> Thee o'er to harshness . . . .
> . . . Thou better know'st
> The offices of nature, bond of childhood," etc.

Mr. Booth sounded the various stops of grief, of parental love, of irony, of indignation, of baffled but clinging hope, which filled interchangeably, or inhabited together in discord, the heart of Lear, until — Goneril enters.

The transcendant art of Shakespeare, in bringing her upon the scene, that the two unnatural daughters may vie with each other in impious speech, so that Lear, heart-struck, if not heart-broken, is torn and cast loose at last from all ties of earth, and stands appealing to the heavens: —

> " You see me here, you gods, a poor old man,
> As full of grief as age."

The responsive art of our actor, who, touched with noble anger, filled with grief and unshed tears, crowned with majesty yet without its lendings — abjured all roofs, after visiting upon those " unnatural hags " the overwhelming energy of his wrath, as he rushes out into the storm!

The final test of an actor's worthiness to delineate this sublime figure, is his power to catch and reproduce the insanity of Lear. Hazlitt says: "Mr. Kean's performance, when the king's intellects begin to fail him, and are at last quite disordered, was curious and quaint, rather than impressive or natural. He driveled and looked vacant, and moved his lips so as not to be heard, and did nothing, and appeared at times as if he would quite forget himself. The spectator was big with expectation of seeing some extraordinary means employed; but the general result did not correspond to the waste of preparation." Dana takes a directly opposite view. He says: "It has been said that Lear is a study for one who would make himself acquainted with the workings of an insane mind. And it is hardly less true that the acting of Kean was an embodying of these workings. There was a childish feeble gladness in the eye, and a half-piteous smile about the mouth, at times, which one could scarce look upon without tears." If this be true, the question still remains, did Kean represent the insanity of

Lear? The phases and modes of mental derangement differ as widely in different persons, as do the operations of the healthful mind. A generalized expression of insanity would hardly suffice for the character we are considering; but this, it would seem, was the sum of Kean's achievement.

The madness of Lear was not a chaos of mind; neither was it a declension towards imbecility. It was an aberration. The imagination was exalted, although diverted from the truth of things; and presented, at times, a grandeur of thought and speech, which has no parallel in dramatic literature. The reasoning power was left intact, even when confusion reigned among the subjects of its exercise. We think the text of Shakespeare, deeply mused upon, will bear out this interpretation. It is certain that the view might have been deduced from Mr. Booth's characterization. In the storm scenes, where Lear, with a Greek vigor of imagination, personifies the elements, addressing them as substantial beings, and with a majesty of self-exaltation, yet dashed with madness, calls them —

> "Servile ministers
> That have with two pernicious daughters" —

leagued against him, the acting of Booth was indescribably grand. What Lamb calls "the contemptible machinery of the storm," was forgotten. It was the tempest in Lear's mind, that Mr. Booth made us conscious of, and this range of his personation reached the topmost height of the actor's art.

His mind played over the minor crazed passages, with the "nimble stroke of quick cross lightning." There was no weakness or vacancy in any word or act. Instead of "a childish feeble gladness in the eye," we saw only the blue light of a speculative madness shifting and shining in his eyes. His sharpened looks, and his keen crazy questioning of Edgar, whom yet he treated with a kind of fraternal tenderness; the visioning eye and airy manner, when dealing with the creations of his brain, —

> "Arraign her first, 'tis Goneril,"

and —

> "Then let them anatomize Regan; see what breeds about her heart" —

if these things did not make us weep, it was because they touched a depth below the source of tears.

In order to avoid a vain repetition of terms,

we touch lightly the pathos of the chamber scene which follows the arrival of Cordelia. His return to soundness of mind, in the appeasing presence of his one true daughter, was as subtle, tender, and graduated, as the departure had been violent and willful. Never, even from his mouth, have we heard a more pathetic utterance, than he gave to the line —

"If you have poison for me I will drink it."

Not only was it filled with music, but with the remorseful humility of a bruised heroic heart.

Our notes on Booth's Lear must here close abruptly. The last scene, the great scene for sounding the inmost depths of human feeling, not only in this play, but in all dramatic literature, was left out. Booth played Tate's Lear. It does not lessen our chagrin to add that Garrick played at an earlier date, and Kean at a later, in that diversion on Shakespeare's grandest drama, which leaves out the indispensable Fool, and puts in the superfluous folly.

We have no fault to find with Booth's Lear so far as he followed Shakespeare. We sat at his feet. But his performance was a magnificent fragment. It might be compared to that *torso* of Hercules, which Angelo so reverently studied, and which conveyed through its knotted and swayed outlines, the suggestion of a grief we may guess at, but which, in its fullness, must remain forever unexpressed.

CASSIUS.

In earlier years Mr. Booth assumed many minor characters of Shakespeare, which he afterwards surrendered, as Richard II., Hotspur, King John, Posthumous. There may still be found in London a print of him in the latter character. Cassius was the last part so surrendered. He played it in Boston, with Mr. Forrest as Brutus, about the year 1837.

Cassius was a Roman, whose subtle mind, restless spirit, and splenetic humor, allied him to the modern Italian, and showed some points of likeness to Iago. But when we name this "Italian fiend," the generous and constant friendship between Brutus and Cassius must of course be put from view. The noble head, the mobile features, the spare figure of Booth gave him a singular external fitness for the part. Perhaps no passage in any performance of his, transcended in colloquial style the well-known street scene with Brutus. His description of himself and Cæsar swimming in the Tiber on that "raw and gusty day;" and of Cæsar's sickness "when he was in Spain," were especially noteworthy. Booth's vivid portraiture recreated the event. He touched the arm of Brutus; leaned, but without undue familiarity, upon his shoulder. In the line —

> "His coward lips did from their color fly,"

Cassius, by a subtle reversion of the common phrase, "the color fled from his lips," implies a sarcasm on Cæsar's quality as a soldier. Booth illustrated the meaning by a momentary gesture, as if carrying a standard. The movement was fine, as giving edge to the sarcasm, but pointed to a redundancy of action, which sometimes appeared in this great actor's personations; marking the excess in him, however, of those high histrionic powers, keen feeling and shaping imagination.

His Cassius was signalized by one action of characteristic excellence and originality. After Cæsar had been encompassed and stabbed by the conspirators, and lay extended on the floor of the Senate-house, Booth strode right across the dead body, and out of the scene, in silent and disdainful triumph.

SIR GILES OVERREACH.

Out of Shakespeare, through Massinger, down to the lowest quarry to which his genius deigned to stoop — to Payne, Colman, Otway, even to Sheil and Maturin, the path of our actor was a track of light; and, against the mass of dramatic dullness it sometimes met,

> "Stuck fiery off indeed."

His "Sir Giles Overreach," in Massinger's play, "A New Way to pay Old Debts," stands in our memory as a representation of singular solid force. We propose to relimn some of the bolder strokes, and hold a candle towards some of the finer touches of this artist's work. When he speaks of having, as servants to his daughter Margaret —

> "The ladies of errant knights decayed,"

he adds, —

> "There having ever been
> More than a feud, a *strange antipathy*
> Between us and true gentry,"

Booth infused into those two italicized words

the aspiring and implacable hatred of the rich and overbearing commoner. His gesture, like his speech, escaped the confinement of rules. It was the natural language of imaginative passion; or the "complement extern" of fine perceptions. In the scene where Sir Giles urges Marrall to work the ruin of Wellborn, and says —

> "Persuade him that 'tis better steal than beg,"

he gave the word "steal" with the fingers of his right hand downward, and as in act of taking: "than beg," palm up, as in act of solicitation — and both movements with rapid ease.

The scene with Margaret, where he tries to induce her to receive, or if need be, catch, the attentions of Lord Lovel, was a masterpiece.

> "If you are my true daughter,
> You'll venture alone with one man, though he came
> Like Jupiter to Semele."

Margaret protests —

> "If to obey you I forget my honor,
> He must and will forsake me."
> *Sir Giles.* "How! Forsake thee!
> Do I wear a sword for fashion; or is this arm
> Shrunk up or withered? Does there live a man,
> Of that large list I have encountered with,
> Can truly say, I e'er gave inch of ground,
> Not purchased by his blood, that did oppose me?"

These lines were so full and bristling with shining points of the actor's art, that we shall attempt an analysis of Mr. Booth's victorious method of rendering them. He uttered "forsake thee!" with a shriek of astonishment.

> "Do I wear a sword for fashion?"

beginning low, and as on a rising wave of passion, the last word blown disdainful, like the foam from its crest. In saying it, he clutched the scabbard with his left hand, and struck the sword-hilt with his right.

> "Or is this arm
> Shrunk up or withered?"

He grasped his outstretched right arm with the fingers of the left hand, and gave the phrase in throated and roughened tones of scorn. The words of the continuing lines were "rammed with life," and full of the solid temper of Sir Giles, down to the word "blood;" when his voice dropped suddenly to its subterranean chamber, and he uttered the phrase "that did oppose me," in a cool depth of tone, which seemed to assure the doom of all antagonists.

Wellborn, cheated and hated of Sir Giles, is presented to him by Lady Allworth, with the remark, "If I am welcome, bid him so." The manner in which Booth stood, with his back turned, betraying an inward strife by subtle motions of head, hands, and features, until, mastering repugnance by policy, he turned suddenly with affected heartiness, and grasped the youth's hand, saying, "My nephew!"—was a most felicitous touch. To Lord Lovel's question if he is not moved by the imprecations of those he has wronged, Sir Giles replies—

> "Yes, as rocks are
> When foaming billows split themselves against
> Their flinty ribs; or as the moon is *moved*
> When wolves, with hunger pined, howl at her brightness."

The change of voice from the howling pack to the silver clearness of the moon, in the words "at her brightness," made the listener feel the assumption of unapproachable serenity. The whole speech was a magnificent example of self-assertion, and suggested how grandly Mr. Booth could have enacted Coriolanus. We do not know that he ever did personate this character; but one night in Cincinnati, when the mood was on, he took down a volume of Shakespeare, and *read* the whole play aloud to his son Edwin.

Lamb's argument that the sight of objects

dispels the imagination of them, is disproved by notable examples. Does not the imagination rather deal with sensible objects, according to its own exalting laws? Fuseli, the painter, said that after reading Chapman's most characteristic translation of Homer, he went out into the street, and the men he met, seemed to him to be ten feet high! Father Hennepin, the first white man who ever looked upon the Falls of Niagara, makes, in his quaint and simple record, the wild surmise, "that they are at least six hundred feet high!" And he bore truer testimony to the spirit of the scene, than does the scientific tourist, who takes the altitude of the cliff in English feet. When Booth, on a certain occasion, as Sir Giles, challenged Lord Lovel, and ran (*not shuffled*) out, but finding he was not followed, came directly back, stood just within the scene, and uttered these words in his deepest voice,

"Are you pale?" —

he took his stature from the mind: his figure seemed to dilate with the vast expansion of his will, and actually to overstate in physical dimension, the bulky and brawny Scotchman who played Lord Lovel.

LUKE.

In Massinger's play entitled the "City Madam," adapted for the modern stage under the name of "Riches," Mr. Booth played the part of Luke. The plot is simple. Luke, a ruined prodigal, is obliged to accept, in order to "keep base life afoot," the situation of servant to his brother's wife, the City Madam. His conduct in this capacity is so exemplary that his brother, believing in the prodigal's reformation, yet willing to test its reality, feigns death, leaving Luke all his immense wealth. The servant turns tyrant, maltreats his former mistress, and is reveling at a feast in solitary luxury, when Sir John appears, as from the dead. Luke, though struck at first with terror, soon comprehends the situation, and dashes from the scene in a rage.

The sight of our actor, a short man in servant's livery, carrying a number of band-boxes and bundles, and scolded by madam for his tardiness, at first provoked a smile. But the manner of gentle reverence, and the intellectual intonation with which he delivered the following speech, soon changed the feeling of the auditor: —

> "I am your creature, madam,
> And if I have in aught offended,
> I humbly ask your pardon.
> But as I was obliged to bring
> These from the Tower, these from the old Exchange,
> And these from Westminster, — I *could* not come
> *Much* — sooner."

Coming from the room filled with riches which he has unexpectedly inherited, he says —

> "I am sublimed, I walk on air!"

not with that epicurism of elocution which the words invite, but with the roughened voice of a man who could not contain his selfish joy.

He presided at his solitary banquet with a kind of Satanic grace. When, in the midst of it, terror at the appearance of his brother gives way to rage, and he dashes past him with the words —

> "Bar not my way! The world is wide enough
> For thee and me,"

he sounded the grand organ stop of his voice, with that easy power, which at once startled and charmed the audience.

SIR EDWARD MORTIMER.

William Godwin, on seeing Booth, at the age of twenty, play Iago, was so struck with his excellence that he wrote the young tragedian a letter, filled with discriminating praise. From Godwin's novel called "Caleb Williams," Colman dramatized the play called the "Iron Chest;" and Mr. Booth's portrayal of the principal character, we have always regarded as one of his most effective personations. We use the adjective with deliberate intent. Effective it was beyond measure, and above praise. Indeed, if it had been our actor's purpose to combine in one representation all the daring, and difficult, and terrific feats, in look, voice, action, of which his supple frame was capable, he could not have selected a better field for the exhibition than this play affords.

Who that ever saw Mr. Booth as Sir Edward Mortimer, can forget his utterance of the name "Adam, Adam Winterton," just before the scene draws, and discloses him seated at his library table? It carried from the invisible speaker the whole tragedy, in its muffled, yet resonant and boding cry. The opening soliloquy of Sir Edward, a sensitive, generous, honorable man, but stained with the guilt of a secret murder, was filled with melancholy beauty. He invokes —

> "That mind of man
> . . . .
> Which lifts us to the stars, which carries us
> O'er the swollen waters of the angry deep,
> As swallows skim the air."

Booth gave, with his picturing voice, the very look of the chafed and billowy sea — then, by a fine ethereal transition, the motion of a bird in air.

The passion of this play is, as the actor once quaintly expressed it, "on the tight jump all the time." Every scene in which Sir Edward appears has a pyrotechnic brilliancy. The interest centres, not in the evolution of character, but in the presentation of special scenes and situations. These were given with wonderful resource of voice and look, and equal vividness and variety of action. Witness for instance the first scene with the secretary, Wilford, who seeks to penetrate his master's secret.

"Sirrah! What am I about?
Oh, Honor! Honor!
Thy pile should be so uniform, displace
One atom of thee, and the slightest breath
Of a rude peasant makes thine owner tremble
For his whole building!"

The rapid changes in voice and manner, in this speech, and the original intonation of the concluding phrase, at once reckless and sustained, and as if the building were about tumbling into ruin, — were marked by Mr. Booth's unique and inimitable method.

No actor we have ever seen seemed to have such control over the vital and involuntary functions. He would tremble from head to foot, or tremble in one outstretched arm to the finger tips, while holding it in the firm grasp of the other hand — as in the last scene of this play, where he says —

"Curse on my flesh to tremble so."

The veins of his corded and magnificent neck would swell, and the whole throat and face become suffused with crimson in a moment, in the crisis of passion, to be succeeded on the ebb of feeling by an ashy paleness. To throw the blood into the face is a comparatively easy feat for a sanguine man by simply holding the breath; but for a man of pale complexion to speak passionate and thrilling words pending the suffusion, is quite another thing. On the other hand it must be observed that no amount of merely physical exertion, or exercise of voice, could bring color into that pale, proud, intellectual face. This was abundantly shown in Shylock, in Lear, in Hamlet, where the passion was intense, but where the face continued clear and pale.

To return to Sir Edward. In the terrible scene in the library, when he proposes the oath of secrecy to Wilford, and —

> "Waxing desperate with imagination,"

reënacts the murder he has confessed; in the threat to Wilford —

> "Dare to make
> The slightest movement to awake my fears,
> And the gaunt criminal naked and stake-tied,
> Left on the heath to blister in the sun
> Till lingering death shall end his agony,
> Compared to thee, shall seem more enviable
> Than cherubs to the damned!"

the accents of which, even to the last reverberant word, ring startlingly clear in our memory — in all this scene no color mantled his face, or mingled in the manifest working of his features. But when old Winterton comes in, and Sir Edward turns to Wilford, fixing him with magnetic glance, and utters the parting admonition —

> "I shall be angry,
> Be very angry if I find you — careless,"

the reiterated word, given in prolonged and kindling tones, carried also a flush of feeling visibly into his face. In a former scene, where he seizes Wilford, and cries out —

> "Slave! I will crush thee! pulverize thy frame,
> That no vile particle of prying nature
> May ——— ha! ha! ha! I will not harm thee, boy,
> O, agony!"

and rushes from the scene, the gust of anger gathers and spends itself without change of color; but the sudden revulsion of feeling that takes place with the words —

> "I will not harm thee, boy,"

crimsons his face and neck with burning shame. His ghastly pallor in the death scene shall conclude this episode on color. In a word, he commanded his own pulses, as well as the pulses of his auditors, with despotic ease.

John Howard Payne, in a published criticism on Booth's Mortimer, speaks happily of the "manual eloquence" he exhibited. The beauty of this hand-play, shone throughout the drama, above the terror of the representation. The indescribable motion of both hands towards those heart-wounds —

> "Too tender e'en for tenderness to touch;"

the creeping, trembling play of his pale, thin fingers over his maddening brain; and his action when describing the assassination, may serve as examples.

A melancholy interest attaches to this part, in view of the fact that it was the last character in which Mr. Booth ever appeared.

BRUTUS.

Mr. Booth was never the literary fashion. He came unheralded, and without letters. He was obliged to introduce himself to the manager of the Richmond theatre, on the occasion of his first performance in this country. He came to Boston and appeared in Colman's play called the "Mountaineers," — "Octavian by Mr. Booth" — to a moderate house. But the fire took, and the next day the town was ablaze with interest in the new tragedian — an interest that scarcely flagged during the following thirty years.

It was the native whim of this monarch of tragedy, to go about incognito; to mix with the people; to play at second-rate theatres. The reward he got, beside that richest and ever sure reward which the artist enjoys in the excellence of his work, was a fullness and heartiness of popular appreciation which our actor felt was infinitely better than the cool approval of scholars. He avoided the listless and fashionable audiences, with the blue blood sleeping in their veins, and who go to the theatre for idle pastime. He turned with joy to crowded audiences of the people with the red blood leaping in their arteries, who went to the theatre to see the play, and him in it; and whom he melted by the pathos, or raised by the grandeur, or charmed by the beauty of his impersonations. If the exclusive, of nice culture, excluded himself from these impersonations, on account of the place in which they shone, or the company who enjoyed their light, then the loss was irreparably his.

The current of our remark brings us to the little "Eagle," a theatre in Boston, about as large as the "Globe" theatre in London in which Shakespeare had a share, and in which Shakespeare played. Good society shunned the "Globe." There is no evidence that Lord Bacon —

> "Large-browed Verulam,"

ever set foot in it. When Shakespeare's company played before the Queen, it was at the palace, and not at the play-house. The "Globe" was not fashionable. Neither was the "Eagle." A few gray heads, whose hearts continued warm; a few critical brains;

a few enthusiastic youths; and the remainder of the little cockpit was filled up by that crowd which the seething city spills after nightfall into its places of amusement. Bounded in that nutshell, Hamlet became king of the infinite spaces of thought; Richard found "ample room and verge enough" for his vast ambition; and there took place the most intense and memorable representation of John Howard Payne's tragedy of Brutus, or the Roman Father.

The playwright found rich material for his work in history and in literature. Junius Brutus, a supposed fool, but hiding his wit through policy, hears from Sextus Tarquin his confession of the ravishment of Lucretia; and breaks out upon him in a speech of fiery indignation. Throwing aside the mask of folly, Brutus incites his countrymen to revenge, and to the extirpation of the Tarquins. He is clothed with civil and military power, and vanquishes the enemy. But his own son, fighting on the side of Tarquin, is taken prisoner. Here centres the chief and closing interest of the play, in the struggle between the duty of the magistrate, and the feelings of the father. In this struggle the Roman triumphs, and Brutus condemns his son to death. The play has supernatural scenes, which are failures; but those scenes which turn on the domestic affections, display unusual power. We believe the tragedy was written expressly for Mr. Booth. It is certain that the author was an intimate and admiring personal friend of the actor.

Booth enters running, and is called by some other character on the scene to minister to his amusement. The rounded back, the blank face, the restless, aimless motion of the hands, enacted folly to the life. Moved by his evil genius, Tarquin reports for pastime to Brutus, the details of his crime, beginning with the remark that he will fill the fool with wonder. Brutus replies —

> "You can say nothing that would make me wonder."

Before the last word he made a slight pause, his looks grew keen, he uttered the word "wonder" with an ominous and penetrating accent, then leaned to listen.

During Tarquin's recital, Booth's eyes kindled with a strange blue light. His back straightened. He stood, crowned with reason, and on fire with indignation; and thus transformed as into a strong avenging angel (Tarquin's story done), he hurled upon him an anathema, the agony of which should last "millions of years."

Never shall we forget that speech. Every fibre of his frame seemed to contribute to swell the energy of his voice. And all the elements of his voice —

> "Constringed in mass,"

burst upon the astonished and terrified offender. Nor can we forget Booth's pale and terrible face, nor the lightning of his glance, nor the unexpected, but most dramatic movement which supplemented the speech. While speaking he stood still, towering above his victim; but after the words "millions of years," he began to stride down the stage. The power which had animated his voice was transferred to his action; and he literally occupied the little stage, treading it transversely to the extreme corner, as if he would pass over among the audience; then turning abruptly, he strode up again to the other extreme, a fearful play of look and feature, betraying meanwhile a silent, inward, growing, and tremendous resolution.

We next find him in the public square, addressing the citizens, over the body of Lucretia. There was no elocution in this speech. It was rough in voice, half choked with feeling. The manner was at the farthest remove from that of an opera singer, listening to his own musical grief. But his tones seemed the outcry of a torn and bleeding heart, and in them a noble anger strove with and finally overmastered the softer emotions.

It is safe to affirm that no passage in any performance of his, either in or out of Shakespeare, exhibited a greater intensity of dramatic conception, or a more thorough accord of utterance and action than did the closing scene of this play. The Roman costume left head, neck, and arms bare. There might be seen swift changes of color ; swifter and subtler movements of head and feature, now quivering and writhing with emotion, now fixed in immovable resolve. To watch this varied movement would have satisfied the deaf. To listen to the accompanying tones, often inarticulate heart-cries, wrung thence by the passion of the hour, would have given mental vision to the blind.

PESCARA.

Shiel, in his play of the "Apostate," wrote the part of Pescara for Booth. Booth responded, by creating the character for Shiel: that is, he poured into its ugly and defective mould his own splendid faculty and abounding life. To speak the interior truth, we think both parties might have been better employed, Shiel in writing, Booth in delineating; for a more desperate example of inhuman depravity than this Pescara, could scarcely be hunted out of literature.

If it be said Iago is more fiendish; we answer, let him be so. The difference of the two characters is a difference of kind. Iago is an intellectual experiment on the part of a capable young man of twenty-eight, to see how successfully he can play the game of life, leaving God entirely out. He is full of subtlety, and many parts of his speeches, as set forth by the unmatched art of Shakespeare, might, when viewed apart from his character, shine in ethical discourse. Pescara, on the contrary, is an uninteresting villain, ventilating bad passions in turgid rhetoric; and holding the attention only by a cruel force of will, exercised in his office as governor of Granada.

Probably, there worked through the dull brain of the author, and out into his dark and cruel Spaniard, some dim reminiscence of Shakespeare's "super-subtle Venetian." Certainly, in the personation of Pescara, Booth drew off some of that spirit which filled his Iago, adulterated it with Shiel, and offered it with great acceptance to the rank palate of a popular audience —

> "Darkening his power to lend base subjects light."

Yet the flashing and magnetic eye; the crisp, resonant, and changeful tones; the natural attitudes of easy power; the lithe strength in action, always characteristic of Booth, — lent their wonted charm to this performance also, and made even Pescara yield a transitory delight.

Two sets of characters figure in the play; Moors and Christians. Pescara is one of the Christians. His first entrance is highly dramatic. Hemeya, a Moor, and his successful rival, is saying to Florinda —

"Who now shall part us?"

"I," replies Pescara, entering. Booth's action, as he stepped upon the scene, had something of the measured force of his first entrance in Richard, and something of the stealthy tread of his Iago; while the word he uttered, gave voice in one little syllable to the whole malign personality of the character.

In a later scene, he was accustomed to recount a dream or vision, in a manner desperately vivid. A lady of much histrionic excellence, told in our hearing, how, as Florinda, in this scene, she involuntarily shrank from his touch, possessed by his ferocious aspect and resounding voice. But he, with that conscious and tactile delicacy, which never left him, even when most filled with the inspiration of his art, in a few low-toned words reassured her, and proceeded without a moment's pause, to possess with his vision the imagination of his auditors. The calm directing mind sat at the centre of his wildest passion, like—

"The whirlwind's heart of peace."

REUBEN GLENROY.

Let us touch a few other characters with a slight pencil. In Colman's play, "Town and Country," Reuben, accompanied by Cosey, is seeking his lost love in the labyrinths of London. The kind old man makes some casual remark, at which the lover winces.

Cosey. "I beg pardon for bringing her to your mind."
Reuben. "*Bringing* — her — to my mind?"

Booth gave the first word with a pathetic ringing clearness, paused slightly before and after "her," and closed the sentence, in a manner very low, clear, and quick; most exquisitely conveying the plain meaning, that she was *always* in his mind.

OCTAVIAN.

Octavian, in the "Mountaineers," is a ragged and melancholy Spaniard, of high birth and breeding, who finds his love, Floranthe, after long and wretched separation, and under extraordinary circumstances.

The deep joy of this discovery was depicted by Mr. Booth with a tender fullness of expression most winning to the popular heart. We also recall one unique gesture. He locked the fingers of his raised hand within the fingers of Floranthe, while speaking, — a subtle and beautiful diversion on that dangerous thing, the stage embrace.

Booth rarely yielded even to the most vociferous call to appear before the curtain. On one occasion, however, in Octavian, at the close of the play, he came towards the footlights as the curtain was descending, let it fall behind him, was still atmosphered by the melancholy beauty of the character, bowed to the audience, and silently withdrew.

BERTRAM.

CLERGYMEN are seldom good playwrights: witness the "Zanga" of Dr. Young, the "Cataline" of Mr. Croly. The old feud between the pulpit and the stage makes it difficult for any combatant to fight, either for love, or fame, or hire, successfully on both sides. The didactic and the dramatic methods of presenting truth, lie respectively at opposite poles: and an author is determined by native temperament or mental constitution towards either one or the other method, but never towards both.

Let this view furnish what excuse it may for the Reverend J. Maturin, who wrote the wretched tragedy of "Bertram." The play is a little worse than the "Apostate," and that is highly unnecessary. Morbid passion, adultery, murder, suicide, mark its criminal progress; and it is choked by a throng of incongruous and unnatural incidents.

Bad as the play is, Booth descended occasionally to its level, and by the touch of his histrionic genius, stirred its corruption into a transient phosphorescent brilliancy. To Bertram, as to Pescara, he contributed himself; and in the enjoyment of his consummate art, we sometimes happily lost sight of the author.

Bertram is picked up from a wreck and borne in on men's shoulders, as one drowned. In his slow recovery of consciousness, Mr. Booth took the spectator with him. One could almost feel the partial flow and quick ebb of the vital current; and the intermittent thrill of life to his extremities. He delivered such passages as —

> "No dews from Heaven fall on this blighted soil,"

and —

> "I have offended Heaven, I will not mock it,"

with a melancholy, undeserved, Byronic grace. We find nothing else in this play worthy to illustrate our subject.

PIERRE.

Mr. Booth's Pierre, in Otway's tragedy of "Venice Preserved," was distinguished by one salient passage of extraordinary energy and clearness. He is urging his fellow conspirators to fire the city of Venice. He stood with his back to the audience, appealing with fierce eloquence to each one of his companions in turn. Well do we remember his transport at the vision of—

> "The Adriatic in her robes of flame."

The last performance of this part that we recall, took place at the Howard Atheneum in Boston, about the year 1847. After the play, we met a gentleman, ripe in years and culture, who had known Mr. Booth throughout his career, and who said he had never seen him exhibit more beauty or clearness of voice and gesture, than on this occasion. The remark acquires value, in view of the "blown surmise," that the actor's voice, if not his general histrionic power, had become impaired by the accident to his face.

THE STRANGER.

Of Kotzebue's play, entitled "The Stranger, or Misanthropy and Repentance," only this remains: the piquant tone and gesture with which he said —

"When they see me with my runaway wife upon my arm."

In considering this play, so weak and so unworthy of representation, the question naturally arises, why did not Mr. Booth enact Timon? We suppose the managers might have answered. We can only regret that he did not add this mighty figure to his Shakespearean gallery. We can only fancy the large and hospitable style he might have lent to the beginning of the play; his impetuous scorn when the tide of prosperity is turning, and the isolated majesty of mien and voice, becoming the sullen grandeur of the closing scenes.

THE TRAGEDIAN.

In the exercise of the most effective and inclusive, if not the most exalted of the fine arts, the art of acting, Mr. Booth's method was

"Unremovably coupled to nature."

The term "theatrical," invidiously used, could never be justly applied to him. Nature was the deep source of his power; and she imparted her own perpetual freshness to his personations. We could not tire of him, any more than we tire of her. His art was, in a high sense, as *natural* as the bend of Niagara; as the poise and drift of summer clouds; the play of lightning; the play of children; or as the sea, storm-tossed, sunlit, moonlit, or brooded in mysterious calm — and his art awakened in the observer corresponding emotions.

AN INCIDENT.

Garrick, in addition to his other gifts, was an admirable dancer. Kean danced ; he also sang exquisitely, employing a faculty not uncommon with rough-speaking men. Booth could neither dance nor sing. The single comic song with which he enlivened his performance in farce, was simply a grotesque jingle, scorning melody, and depending for its success on odd turns of expression, verbal and vocal. We recall a true incident, showing his characteristic admiration of a talent he did not possess.

After a splendid success in tragedy, he stood at the wing (as at other times, on going behind the scenes, we have seen him stand), with folded arms, in the dress of the character he had just personated, and listening intently to an excellent singer, then before the audience. Unable to congratulate him at the time, Booth sought and found the singer, later in the night, at a refreshment room in company with other actors. Booth entered the room, silently stretched himself at full length upon the sanded floor, took one of the singer's feet, placed it upon his own neck, held it so a few moments, then rose and departed without word.

A DIALOGUE.

SCENE. — *A hotel chamber, dimly lighted. Time — summer evening. Mr. Booth discovered sitting at an open window, smoking. A glazed cap, and a roundabout formed a part of his dress, giving him the appearance of a "Middy Ashore." Enter Guest. Interchange of salutations and courtesies.*

Guest. I saw your "Sir Giles" last evening. How do you manage to carry the scene so smoothly, with such weak support?

Actor. By close attention to the business of the stage.

Guest. But you seemed to lose yourself in your impersonation.

Actor. Else how could I identify character?

Guest. And can you keep up these two diverse processes of thought at the same time?

Actor. Nothing easier — after the machinery is oiled. In one view, that is a strange play, — "A New Way to pay Old Debts," — not one honest person in it. They are all rogues from beginning to end; rogues for virtue, rogues in vice. Shakespeare drew the foibles of the good; but he never blurred the lines, by making the good counterplot against the villains. Did you see how near they came to letting Shakespeare's birthplace slip into the hands of a Yankee speculator? I once saw, on the 23d of April, the whole way from London to Stratford lined with flowers, in honor of the poet. They should preserve every vestige of him.

Guest (Murmurs the title of a book then popular). "Vestiges of Creation."

Actor (Catching the allusion, instantly rejoins). Yes, he was the god of the histrionic art in England. Can you tell me whether Howard Payne be still living?

Guest. I cannot. But I recall a *bon mot* upon him, made by some London critics, who "cut up" his tragedy of Brutus. The author was indiscreet enough to retort through the press. Whereupon the critics rejoined, —

"The labor we delight in, physics Payne."

and turned the laugh on him. Mr. Booth, did you ever read in public?

Actor. Reading is emasculate acting. The drama should never be so treated. (Then added, smiling) I did attempt it once. I read the "Ancient Mariner" at the Chatham Street Theatre in New York. But the reading was a failure. The boys were cracking nuts and calling out to each other, "Hi! hi!" all over the house.

Guest. I fear your audience was of similar quality to those sailors, who are said to have bought up the first edition of the poem, out of regard to the name. But they soon became disgusted with the purchase. They couldn't fathom the meaning. "I would I had been there," and heard your reading, even with the "Hi! hi!" accompaniment.

Actor (whiff, whiff, in silence).

Guest. How vivid the imagery, how alluring the measure of that remarkable poem.

"The fair breeze blew, the white foam flew;
The furrow followed free."

Actor (continuing the verse).

"We were the first that ever burst,
Into that silent sea!"

Guest (Listens patiently, but hears no more of the "Ancient Mariner" that night. The actor was "not i' the vein").

Actor. The reports about Rachel interest me greatly. She has become famous since my last visit to Europe. The French style, even in the antiquated tragedy of Racine, is closer to nature than ours.

Guest. Is she a Jewess?

Actor. Juive Francaise (with exquisite purity of accent). By the way, this is the first Jewish month (September).

Guest takes leave.

Actor. Come down with me to supper; come, take a bit. I'm going in (on the stairs). Come now, you'd better take a bit.

Guest declines, bids good-night, and sees the actor pass across the hall, and out of sight, with his natural and kingly stride.

His knowledge and accent of the French tongue were simply perfect. He played Oresté in Racine's tragedy, "Andromaque," at the French Theatre in New Orleans, repeatedly, and in a manner to rouse the wildest enthusiasm. Frenchmen of that city speak of him to this day, as a second Talma.

Meeting on one occasion, at the house of the late Governor Andrew, a select company of gentlemen and ladies, the talk turned on the stage and the drama, and was varied by imitations running up into the region of Shakespearean criticism. The Reverend Mr. Clarke, who was present, related an adventure he had with Mr. Booth in Louisville. His recital was the germ of an excellent paper, which has since appeared in the Atlantic Monthly. At the close of the interview therein described, and which appears so full of histrionic, eccentric, and psychological interest, the player told the preacher that he had called on him as a Unitarian, a monotheist, himself being a Jew. Whether the latter statement referred to race or religion, is left a little uncertain.

Nothing can be surer, however, than that Mr. Booth's mind was deeply exercised by religious problems; by "obstinate questionings" of futurity and human destiny. The chance companions of his convivial hours, or even the thrilled auditor and spectator of his matchless impersonations, could have had little conception of this, his private and habitual mood.

He passed into all religions with a certain humility and humanity, and, we may add, with a certain Shakespearean impartiality. Among Jews, he was counted a Jew. He was as familiar with the Koran as with the Hebrew Scriptures, and would name a child of his after a wife of Mahomet. At other times, and in sympathy with his favorite poet, Shelley, he delighted to lose himself in the mysticism of the faiths of India.

THE TRAGEDIAN.

In recording our impressions of him, who, if power of identification be the actor's supreme gift, was perhaps the greatest of all actors, we have lived over again hours of rare æsthetic delight. We indulge the hope that this happiness has been in some measure communicated to the reader.

But the play is over. The curtain has fallen; the actor vanished. His voice is hushed. Its wild bell has died upon the air. His eye is quenched. No more shall the quick imagination of Shakespeare,—

> "Fill its blue urn with fire."

That organization, so elastic, firm, dense, fibrous, delicate, has become a pinch of dust. Yet remains the indestructible hope, that, out of the—

> "Abysmal deeps of personality,"

—how, when, or under what aspect, who can tell?—himself shall arise immortal and sacred still to the beneficent ministry of beauty.

www.ingramcontent.com/pod-product-compliance
Lightning Source LLC
LaVergne TN
LVHW011216110826
845150LV00006B/1444

* 9 7 8 1 4 2 5 5 1 6 9 2 5 *